CE-5

Initiating Contact with Extraterrestrials

By Peter Maxwell Slattery

CE-5 Initiating Contact with Extraterrestrials

© 2021 by Peter Maxwell Slattery

Cover by Kesara (Christine Dennett), www.kesara.org

Editor: Jessica Bryan, www.oregoneditor.com

DISCLAIMER: The information in this book is intended to be of a general educational nature, and does not constitute medical, legal, or other professional advice for any specific individual or situation.

No part of this book may be reproduced or transmitted in any form or by any means without permission in writing from the publisher.

Published by Peter Maxwell Slattery

Email: petermaxwellslattery@gmail.com

Website: www.petermaxwellslattery.com

ISBN: 978-1-716-30468-2

DEDICATION

This book is dedicated to all Beings throughout all planes and in-between, throughout the universe and beyond.

THANK YOU!

A big thank you goes out to my family, friends, and all my supporters and fellow Beings from the many realms in this universe and beyond, for their love and support, and I also thank Shi-Ji.

Also, a big thank you to James Gilliland for his friendship, guidance, support, and for being a mentor to me.

Thank you to all those who are doing the work and assisting with the E.T. reality by spreading the awareness of it and the greater aspect of mind, body, spirit, and that we are all one consciousness. I also thank the health, food, fitness, and science and technology communities.

Thank you to those in the CE-5 community, and to all the groups out there who are educating the world on the E.T. reality.

Love, light, and bliss,

Peter Maxwell Slattery

WARNING

Peter Maxwell Slattery is not responsible for anything that occurs or manifests while practicing the techniques mentioned in this book.

Do not attempt these methods while under the influence of drugs or alcohol.

TESTIMONIALS

JASON GLEAVES (EX-ROYAL AIR FORCE AND BRITISH AEROSPACE) IMAGE ANALYSIS EXPERT ON PETER MAXWELL SLATTERY

– Excerpt from Jason Gleaves' Findings

I am 100% convinced of the authenticity of the images and quality, upon closer analysis of the Aerial Phenomenon captured. When enlarged and enhanced to their visual capacity, they reveal astonishing detail and structure of the UFOs, which vary in shape and color spectrums, ranging from disk-shaped objects to cylindrical/cigar shaped anomalies, plus a few unusual in appearance, certainly not the standard conventional civilian or military aircraft we know and see in our skies today.

Pete's detailed analysis of the visual manifesting of various races of extraterrestrial Beings is simply some of the best I've worked on and seen. He is in the top 1% of authentic experiencer cases in Ufology to-date.

– Jason Gleaves (Ex-Royal Air Force and British Aerospace) –
Ufonly

REMOTE VIEWER JOHN VIVANCO
ON PETER MAXWELL SLATTERY

I have run teams of Remote Viewers on projects for the corporate and intelligence worlds for over twenty years as a professional Remote Viewer. Employing the same methodology I use for gathering information professionally, I rely on Pete Slattery and what he has filmed. In the realm of anomalous film footage, experiences, and knowledge, Pete is one to watch. He is an attractor of both UFO and paranormal phenomena; he has some of the best truly anomalous footage I have ever seen; and our remote viewing projects have determined the legitimacy of what he continually experiences and captures.

– John Vivanco, Professional Remote Viewer
righthemispheric.com

ALLISON COE ON PETER MAXWELL SLATTERY

Wow! Peter's session was so powerful. I was brought to tears numerous times during his reading. He asks for your intention and some questions you're seeking guidance on. To get these answers he has a gift of accessing information beyond the human 3D blueprint, while calling forth the galactic team members who are most of service to you now. Unbeknownst to him, he validated several experiences I had prior to our session. He then empowered me to connect to my guides and team members by giving me access to some tools he has honed through years of his own practice.

The detailed notes he provided post-session have helped me move along the trajectory these messages foretell. This reading came at a time when I needed it most, and I am so honored to have spent the time and money for this priceless reading. Peter has a gift, and I will be sure to use it well into the future. I wish I had known more about Pete, as I would have signed up for one of his workshops in a heartbeat if I had a clear schedule. In Peter, we are getting a glimpse of where human evolution is heading.

–Allison Coe - **QHHT, BQH**

soulfocus-hypnosis.com

JAMES GILLIAND ON PETER MAXWELL SLATTERY

Peter's work in the field of Ufology is paramount and of the highest integrity. His courage and tenacity are reflected in his work. His ability to connect with higher dimensional Beings and film and document them is unsurpassed.

–James Gilliland, ECETI

eceti.org

"The total number of minds in the universe is one."

– Erwin Schrödinger

"The Mind you seek is the mind you connect with."

– James Gilliland

Contents

Overview..17

Part 1 – Introduction..19

    1. What is CE-5?...20
    2. Things to Consider...22
    3. Clearing Techniques......................................30
    4. Preparation..37

Part 2 – Techniques and Tools for Making Contact..........44

    5. Meditation..45
    6. Remote Viewing..53
    7. Connect with Your Spirit Guides and E.T.s.............69
    8. Thought Projection Technique......................81
    9. The Pendulum Technique.............................82
    10. Psychometry Exercise.................................84
    11. Equipment and Its Purpose........................85
    12. Filming Techniques...................................108
    13. Our stuff, Their Stuff................................112
    14. Physical Evidence.....................................115

15. Crafts and Beings Appearing in Ways You Might Not Expect..118

16. Types of ETs and Beings..121

Part 3 – Making Contact..125

17. Preparation: Location and Doing It Alone or as part of a Team..126

18. Safety and Hazards Check..132

19. Tips and Tools..133

20. Setting Up Your Equipment....................................135

21. Energy Work: Connecting Mind, Body, and Spirit..138

22. Initiating Contact...139

23. CE-5 Contact Meditation and Remote Viewing Method..142

24. What to Be on the Lookout For..............................150

25. Examples of Contact Evidence...............................153

26. Ending Your CE-5 Session......................................163

27. Final Note..166

Books by Peter Maxwell Slattery..167

About the Author..168

Overview

This book is a step-by-step guide to initiating contact with otherworldly Beings. Included are photos of what to be on the lookout for, recommended equipment, locations and tips, safety and hazard checks, meditations, notes, and techniques, plus many other tips and tools to assist you with making contact with extraterrestrials. I call this process "CE-5" (Close Encounters of the 5th kind).

These days, Dr. Greer is known for the CE-5 protocols and for the term "CE-5," as well as my good friend James Gilliland, who sponsors ambassador workshops at the famous ECETI Ranch. Many are engaged in this process worldwide, and they are getting results, even if they are doing it in their own way.

Through being in this community for a long time, I have come across people who have been doing something similar to CE-5 going back to the 1960s.

This book discusses my approach to initiating contact, although I recommend researching other people's work and trying different techniques from different sources in order to find out what works for you.

This book is divided into three parts. Part 1 is an introduction to CE-5. Part 2 goes into techniques and tools, and Part 3 discusses a step-by-step process about how you can go about making contact individually or in a group.

I hope you enjoy this book.

In light,

Peter Maxwell Slattery

Part 1

Introduction

1. What is CE-5?

"CE-5" stands for "Close Encounters of the Fifth Kind." This term was added to the original scale created by J. Allen Hynek, who worked on Project Blue Book from 1952 to 1970, (the U.S. Government investigation into UFOs).

The first four possible encounters include:

Close Encounter of the 1st Kind (CE-1) - Observation of a UFO (Unidentified Flying Object) within 500 feet.

Close Encounter of the 2nd Kind (CE-2) – Trace evidence of a landing or physical effects are found after an experience.

Close Encounter of the 3rd Kind (CE-3) – An observation takes place of humanoids/otherworldly Beings that can be associated with a UFO sighting or experience.

Close Encounter of the 4th Kind (CE-4) – Communication and/or an interaction takes place with humanoids/otherworldly Beings, either on or off-board a craft.

Close Encounter of the 5th Kind (CE-5) – A Human (or Humans) initiates contact with E.T.s /otherworldly Beings, resulting in a UFO sighting/experience that includes an interaction on some level with the occupants of the craft and/or otherworldly Beings.

2. Things to Consider

This book is designed to help you initiate contact with otherworldly Beings through the use of conscious/non-linear mind. Also included are tips, tools, and techniques.

Nothing is guaranteed to happen from using these tips and tools, although these techniques have gotten repeatable results for myself and those who have come with me on sky watches, expeditions, and workshops.

It's not about summoning crafts, but rather connecting with otherworldly Beings (if they are willing) and setting the stage for universal peace. It's about creating a dialogue to get acquainted and have a relationship with the greater family of man. This can ultimately lead to connecting with your own God Self and your multidimensional self/mind, although some of you might have done so already and had a God Consciousness or E.T. otherworldly experience before attempting CE-5. This is great, because it can make the process outlined here easier.

The tools mentioned in this book are designed to help open the gate and allow possibility of contact in whatever form, depending on the person, intention, and if you are coming from a place of love and universal peace.

These techniques can help those who want to initiate contact individually or as a group. Love, good intentions, and an open mind are good ways to live, but they are especially important when attempting these techniques.

With that said, I need to be responsible and say that some adverse and unexpected events might result from opening the door to the greater mind of man, the universe, and beyond.

These can be of a positive nature, or what you might perceive as negative. Your lifestyle might change; you might become more in-tune with nature and those around you. The direction of your life and your values can change, and you might wish you had never looked into these topics! Past traumas, wrong conclusions, and judgments can come up – an epiphany of how your life has played out, as well as many other things.

It's like a new you comes into play, and it can be very uncomfortable. But like I say, "To evolve, we have to get out of our comfort zone, because what's waiting on the other side is more amazing and beautiful than we can imagine."

Fear of the unknown and insecurity hold many people back, however, taking a chance is the first step in creating change that offers a whole new world of experience – if you are willing to give it a try.

I must mention that I am a big advocate of "clearings." By this, I am referring to a technique performed through intention and visualization/imagination (Imagination that is really creation). This technique can be used to clear your space, your mind, and your energy field (your Merkabah/Light Vehicle).

Clearings are very important, because when you open up to interact with the greater family of man, Angels, E.T.s, Inner Earth Beings, Gaia, nature spirits, and elementals, etc., you could be opened up to anything and everything if you don't know what you're doing. You might accidentally invite undesirable Beings to come in, including demonic, Archonic, reptilian, or lower light energies.

So… in this book we will be covering clearings, because when we are first awakening our ugly side might come forward as a result of our past experiences. Clearings can assist us with eliminating old emotional patterns and heal the past – and everything else that no longer serves us.

I have to also be responsible and say that attacks can come in many forms, when opening the door. I wish that when I had my awakening many years ago, someone had told me about clearings and what to be on the lookout for.

When we do this inner work, our light shines – the light that is inside each and every one of us. On the astral plane/the blueprint to this reality, the positive Beings out there can "read" you instantaneously. They see everything about you, your past actions and intentions, and they have only love and compassion for you. They are nonjudgmental and they are of service.

On the flip side, those I call "Beings of the Lower Light" see the light we emanate, and they want to stop it from shining. If you experience an unusual or uncomfortable energy because of interference by the Lower Light, it's best to remain calm, do a prayer and/or clearing, and send love to the energy. This is a simple remedy, but it is very effective. Beings of the Lower Light want you to freak out because your negative emotional reaction is like a drug to them.

Psychic attacks can sometimes happen. Out of the blue, you might think of something negative that happened years ago, and as a result you re-experience negative emotions for hours on end. In this case, a negative Being or energy might have read your mind and found something they know will produce fear or frustration in you. They will try to keep you in a negative thought loop so they can feed off your negativity. Sometimes they do it simply to derail you.

At other times, the lower light Beings might try to work through your loved ones and make them say and do things designed to get a negative response from you, even though they are unaware of why. They might think, "Why did I say or do that?"

Again...it all comes back to doing a clearing and observation, rather than getting lost in your reactionary mind. Simply pray, do a clearing, and come from a place of love.

The negative is also an aspect of Source, God, Creator, whatever you want to call it. Negativity exists to show us how to evolve our consciousness and rise above being in reactionary mind. From this positive place, the lower energies can't affect us much, as we move higher in consciousness. In effect, the darkness helps us evolve our consciousness to the point nothing can disturb us.

Now...I'm not saying you will be attacked nightly, daily, or all the time, but every now and then, as you become more sensitive and go through what I call "self-mastery," these things can happen. I do come across people and situations in which some people are so strong they never allow it into their reality, meaning the darkness, so there are exceptions.

This is not to deter you from doing CE-5, or any other practices, but it would be irresponsible of me if I didn't mention these things.

God is within you, and understanding that the mind behind the mind observing the breath is key to doing the practices in this book, in order to make contact with otherworldly Beings and your own God Self.

We are all one consciousness, but we are trying to find ourselves again as we work our way through the illusion of separateness. The truth is you are all that is, and this book is but a step to assist you with reconnecting to your true nature.

This process also comes with the responsibility of being an Ambassador of Humanity to the greater family of man, and to start a dialogue with these beautiful otherworldly Beings, not just individually, but as a group, as a collective. Individual contact comes with this, and for some this is the first step, followed by collective contact and sometimes vice versa.

Also, the otherworldly Beings are not to be looked up to, or to be seen as Gods, or better than us, but as part of the greater family of humanity and as another aspect of ourselves. We are joining our individual and collective mind in a dialogue with these amazing Beings out in the cosmos and beyond.

This is the starting phase, and the time we are in now is a time of being introduced to these Beings on a large, public scale. As someone who is in face-to-face contact with many Beings, whether in a physical or non-physical state, the discussion in this book is just the start of what lies ahead – before we go to the stars in a public arena, as well as the many beautiful realms beyond.

Remember, the greatest technology and portal to experiencing all that is lies within us. It's the light within you, your true nature, who you really are. It all starts within.

3. Clearing Techniques

How to clear negative energies, entities, attachments, and more

As I stated previously, clearings are very important. I do them on and off throughout my day. It's become second nature.

Now what are clearings? Well...as I was saying...a clearing is basically a way to clear negativity and stress from your energy field and your emotions, mind, and physical body. This practice can come in handy in many ways.

Clearings eliminate negative thoughts and experiences, and they also help when you feel stressed or anxious. You can also clear projects or activities, before traveling and before getting into or when in a car, plane, etc. You can do them when you are sick or others around you are sick, upset, or sad, and yes, you can do them for other people or those involved in situations that you feel need them – although I always talk to the person's higher self (their soul) first, and ask if they will except my help with clearing, or not.

Clearings can also help with psychic attacks, or when you experience a negative Being. It's important to add that there are not only what people perceive as negative and/or positive Beings. There is also something in the middle, which I call a "trickster."

Trickster Beings can be positive and/or negative, and if you experience one you will have a positive or negative experience. Sometimes they will just interact with you, but however you encounter them the experience and/or information you receive will come to you through thought transfer (telepathy), and it will be nonsensical. So be aware of this, too.

Now...you don't have to do a clearing exactly the way it is written in this book. You can use prayer, mantras, and singing bowls, burn sage, or envision yourself in a ball of light. There are many techniques that can be effective.

This book is not concrete in how everything needs to be done to get results. It's about showing you tips and tools and incorporating them into your own ideas and finding what works for you, and which can give you repeatable results. But as you find your own ways of doing these practices, always keep an open mind. Be open to new ideas. Continue learning and discovering more tools, so you can expand your "tool box," so to speak.

The clearing technique here, or your own form of it, needs to be done before you meditate, remote view, or initiate contact, although, like I say, do what works for you; create your own technique.

If you open up and invite just anything to connect, without discrimination, you will have no control over what comes in, positive or negative. But by doing a clearing beforehand you can control your environment and your experience, so that only what is aligned with you and your highest good can connect and create a dialogue.

Have fun with this, use your imagination, and go with the flow. The Beings have a great sense of humor. They are loving and insightful, and they have personalities and feelings, just like you.

As I say, would you rather be hanging out with fun and exciting people, or people who are negative, dark, and depressing. So be happy and joyful when going into CE-5 – Initiating Contact with otherworldly Intelligences, because this will amplify your positive results.

CLEARING TECHNIQUE

Start by imagining yourself engulfed in white, golden, violet, or blue-colored light; use whatever colored light you prefer. Then say words that work for you, silently or out loud. Here are examples of the words I use:

1. I ask those who are aligned with the healing of the Earth and the awakening of humanity to connect to my consciousness.

2. I ask the native spirits in my area and Gaia (Mother Earth) to connect to my consciousness. I ask also for their blessing to be here.

3. I ask the nature spirits and elementals that are in alignment with me to connect with my

consciousness.

4. I now ask my Guides, the Masters, Saints, Sages, the Beings I work with, and my own God Self to connect with my consciousness.

5. I also ask that any psychic bonds and connections that are not positive to be dissolved, along with any negative implants and attachments.

6. I ask the healing energies to step forward and assist with any physical, mental, or emotional healing I might need.

7. Let anything that is not in alignment with me be escorted by their guides to where they need to go, and let them know they do not have

to exist in the state they are in—because they are loved, healed, and forgiven.

Finally, blast yourself again with whatever colored light you choose.

Here is a prayer that can be done as a quick form of clearing or for extra support:

Pete's Unbounded Prayer

I call upon the Lords of Light
to take all Beings to the Light.
Let them know they are healed and free.
Blessed they are. So may it be.

4. Preparation

The information in this book is designed to assist you with opening the gate for contact to happen. I suggest (if you don't already do it) that you start meditating – not just to initiate contact, but for spiritual development. Make it part of your daily routine.

A lot of people get bored with meditation because they are unable to clear the mind. No wonder they get bored. But clearing your mind is just a small part of it.

Many meditation teachers and practitioners don't realize that sometimes you need think about where your thoughts come from, and how you perceive what you hear and think.

You can also meditate on situations, ask for guidance and connect with otherworldly Beings. This includes Beings who live amongst us – whether they are on the surface of the earth or inside the earth; in this dimension or not, nature spirits, interdimensional Beings, time travelers (although time is an illusion), spirit guides, your higher self, and the God Source. You can even download information, have it communicated to you telepathically, or leave your body and end up on the astral plane and other physical places, planes, and dimensions, and even Source (God).

Wherever you go and whatever comes through is meant to, so don't worry about where you go or what you do. Just "go with the flow" and let whatever happens continue to happen. Yep…it might sound crazy, but this is the reality of our abilities and our interdimensional mind and consciousness.

Meditation is also a tool (and a valuably one at that) for taking control and being responsible and accountable for creating our own reality. Using this tool, you can learn to let go of the ego, be open-minded, and connect to oneness.

As long as you have good intentions, have a good vibe, and are open-minded and want to do it, you're halfway to making contact. You might have already made contact and don't know it. It's really as simple as "ask, and you shall receive."

You see…we are all one consciousness interacting with itself, and the form of communication all Beings use on an interdimensional and universal level is *thought*. In this way, we are all part of the God/Source, which is all that is, throughout all planes and dimensions. In other words, we are all cells of the same "body." When viewed in this way, you can see how initiating contact with otherworldly Beings is possible. It's rather like the Internet. You send out a message and your intended recipient receives it and responds.

If you understand this, you are on the path to understanding how consciousness/thought can communicate with any Being or Beings, because all points in space and time are connected.

Thought is directed through intention. Those who pick up on the thought transmission are meant to, and they will be Beings that are in service mode – assuming you are coming from a place of love and you have done your clearings.

What I am trying to do, besides help you make contact, is to help you make your own connection with your higher self, God/Source, and otherworldly Beings, individually and as a group.

Now...if you have not meditated before, this book contains instructions about the main points of how to mediate. You can also go to many places on the Internet to download meditation instructions, as well.

It's all about what works for you and doing it your own way. What's here is just an idea of the way I sometimes do it, so look around and find what works for you.

In addition, just like in everyday life, I recommend you get regular exercise, eat a healthy diet, and stay balanced, including hobbies, time alone, social time, time with your partner, kids, and friends, and in your work life.

A balanced life is a productive life. Meditation, in and of itself, does not mean you will become enlightened, however, balancing all areas of your life and having a respectful attitude towards yourself, others, the earth, and the universe is a good start to evolving.

I must also stress that *it's important to invite only enlightened Beings to connect with you. Do not make demands of them.* It's equally important to dissolve all psychic connections with anything or any Being having negative intent. Always be sure to first clear the energy in the space and overall environment where you are planning to meditate, ask only enlightened Beings to connect, and tell anything negative to dissolve.

Some people do not do this and, as a result, they have negative experiences. When someone tells about a negative experience they had during a meditation session, and I ask if they did a clearing before the session, they usually say "no."

Your desire to initiate contact creates the possibility and the reality for it to happen. Doing the meditations in this book can actually help cause an experience to occur, so you're already on the way there. Just remember that all enlightened Beings from many planes and dimensions are highly aware and they can pick up on your intentions. They also know what you are ready for.

If you are not ready, or are not doing it for the right reasons, don't be surprised if nothing happens.

Also, I recommend that you not abuse the ability to initiate contact. Yes...there are many Beings out there, but we need to connect with those we are meant to, and we shouldn't take advantage of this or see the family from beyond being able to solve all our problems.

You might want to meditate in a group, but for your own spiritual development, I recommend doing it alone, at first, in order to work on yourself. If the others you have chosen to do contact work with also meditate and work on themselves as much as you do, then come together to meditate as a group. By creating group consciousness, you will have a greater impact and better results than when you practice alone.

The meditations in this book can be done when initiating contact individually or in a group. If you have not had contact before, the great thing is that after doing a group contact session, you will be able to have experiences by yourself. Actually, you will probably realize that you have been connected all along.

If you are already an experiencer, these meditations can you help create a group contact experience and add to what you already know. You might decide to have both individual and group contact experiences in order to evolve spiritually.

Many people are doing CE-5 and are helping the process for contact as a civilization and to assist in the evolution of all.

The truth of the matter is that we have all lived on other planets, in other dimensions, and so forth – we have just forgotten it. We wake up when we are meant to, and now is the time for us to slowly open our eyes and let our eyes adjust, focus, and really see who we are, where we are from, and what we are capable of.

Part 2

Techniques and Tools for Making Contact

5. Meditation

Meditation is a spiritual practice that uses various techniques and methods through which we can increase our awareness and extrasensory perception. Meditation allows the mind to rest, as we focus inwardly and reach a state of peace in which we are non-reactive to our environment and others around us. In meditation, we connect within to higher level of consciousness.

When looking into connecting with the spirit and extraterrestrial realms, we need to recognize that our consciousness is plugged into the same consciousness as these Beings. Everything is a manifestation of the same consciousness, and if we are open to making meditation our daily practice, even for 15 minutes a day, there are many benefits to be had – including the benefit of connecting with the spiritual realms. Meditation also offers healing emotionally and physically, and helps create balance of mind, body and spirit. It raises our positivity and productivity, and allows us to rest in non-reactionary mind.

For all intents and purposes, in this book I'm going to make this short, simple, and sweet, which is really the way it is and should be. Evolution through meditation shouldn't be complicated, although as humans this can sometimes be the case.

FOLLOW THE BREATH

There are many ways to enter into a state of meditation. Focusing your attention on your breath is a good way, especially when starting out, and even after you become advanced. This practice has many benefits; you can slow down your heart rate and quiet your mind. Observing the breath also connects you to your higher consciousness because it removes you from a state of "mind chatter."

This practice is very easy. Simply breathe in, hold your breath for 3 or 4 seconds, and then breathe out and hold for 3 or 4 seconds. Because you are focusing on your breath, you are not paying attention to your mind chatter and other distractions. Assuming you have done a clearing before beginning to meditate, you might be surprised by the guidance from spirit that can come through.

Now...I want to make this fun, so when I'm referencing imagining something, remember, imagining is creating. It has a purpose. If you don't understand this, at first, know you will, in time. Everything plays out and comes to be understood when you are ready, not beforehand. Spiritual evolution is a process and there are necessary steps to be taken.

Some people fall asleep during meditation. If this happens to you, don't fight it, because sometimes an experience or guidance in the dream state/ lucid dream state, or an astral experience can occur.

Go through the technique below with an open attitude. Don't get deterred or discouraged if nothing happens. The most important aspect is your positive intention; sometimes progress takes time and patience.

Just observe any thoughts, impressions, feelings, and visions that come through in your mind's eye, and simply observe.

In addition to the suggestions here, you might want to go online and find guided meditations that can help you and keep you focused.

If your progress seems slow, perhaps your guides, your higher self, E.T.s, Angels, and other such Beings might be trying to help you bring up thoughts and feelings that need to be healed, purged, and forgiven. You might need to get angry or cry for yourself or others for no apparent reason. This can be part of the release process.

MEDITATION TRAINING TECHNIQUE

Imagine breathing in golden white light.

As I said previously, breathe in, hold for 3 to 4 seconds; then breathe out and hold for 3 to 4 seconds.

As you breathe out, let go of all your troubles and worries. Continue breathing in and out this way until you feel calm. This process will clear your energy.

Next, invite all of the saints, sages, masters, and enlightened Beings from all planes of existence to come in. Finally, tell anything of a self-serving or negative nature that it is not welcome.

Request healing for others and yourself (as needed) and then set the intent to connect with your own God Self.

Imagine a golden white light orb in the middle of your chest. This orb is your own God Self (a cell of Source). Then imagine it getting bigger and bigger, until it engulfs your entire body.

By this time, you might be totally blissed out, but just continue to set your intention for contact at whatever level is appropriate.

Understand that everything of a positive nature that is meant to happen will happen because of the clearing technique you did at the start.

Finally, sit back and rest in peace. When you are ready, bring yourself out of meditation, enjoy the energy, and keep the intent going as you relax, wherever you might be.

TIP – OBSERVATION EXERCISE

To help advance your awareness and observation abilities, I recommend putting on a blindfold and/or putting in earplugs. Then either lie down or sit up for 15 minutes, and observe any sensations you are aware of, including visions in your mind's eye, thoughts, feelings, smells, sounds, and tastes, etc.

I follow this practice for 40 minutes to an hour every day, in addition to meditation and other practices. In this way, you can deprive your hearing and visual senses, which will enable you to observe the other senses in the five-sense reality, as well as the extra two, the mind's eye and thought.

In the next chapter, we are going to take this to the next level with remote viewing. Note, however, the method I discuss here is different than the methods used by most people.

6. Remote Viewing

Remote viewing is a core practice that can help significantly when it comes to CE-5 and initiating contact and interfacing across the dimensions with other worldly intelligences. Remote viewing is closely aligned with meditation.

So...what is it?

Remote viewing is a technique whereby the "viewer" is given a "target" (usually previously unknown to the viewer.) What I mean by "target" is a person, situation, or a place and time of an event. To designate the target, on a piece of paper or on a photo draw a line to the event or target that you would like remote viewed. Then write two sets of four numbers at the other end of the line. These can be any random numbers. Seal the paper inside of an envelope and write the same two sets of four digits on the outside of the envelope.

The remote viewer then writes the numbers down at the top of a piece of paper, followed by an ideogram, which is just a squiggle done intuitively, Basically this connects the remote viewer on a conscious, body level to the target. Next, the viewer writes the first thing that comes to mind, such as colors, objects, smells, and tastes, etc.

Basically, when the remote viewer writes down the numbers, it marks the target with a code, thus creating a link on a consciousness level to the target. This is also a way for the human body/mind to tap into universal consciousness, because the person gave the target a number. From there, the viewer writes down the colors they perceive, objects, dimensions of objects, smells, and tastes, etc.

For example, a military installation might be the target, and the person who set the target might want to know what's inside and around the installation. The remote viewer might draw a warehouse from an aerial view, and a truck inside the warehouse, people, and then a crate. They might observe and write down that there are weapons inside the crate. Later, when looking at the photo inside the envelope, it might show a warehouse.

Here is a step-by-step process for remote viewing:

1. A photo, picture, or words representing an object, person, place, or event is chosen; a line is drawn from the object and given two sets of four digits at the other end of the line.
2. The image is then put into an envelope, and the same two sets of four digits are written on the outside of the envelope.
3. Then it's handed to the viewer.
4. Next, the viewer writes the two sets of four digits at the top of blank piece of paper, followed by a intuitive squiggle – don't think about this; just do it. Sometimes the target might be seen or in a weird way resemble the target.

5. Finally, write down the first thing that comes to mind, including any impressions, such as colors, objects, dimensions of objects, smells, and tastes, etc.

Go with the first thing that comes to mind; if you are in doubt about something (on a section of the page) write "AOL," meaning "Analytical Overlay." This will indicate where you might be off the target and making up what you think you are seeing at the time. This is basically the analytical mind coming through. Either way, write down what comes to mind, because there might be something to it. Then drop the pen; this is a way of resetting the mind and consciousness connection. Then continue.

As you do this, if you start drawing objects or even draw a map intuitively, you can start to refine and zoom in on places you feel are important. Use another piece of paper; skip the target numbers and ideogram, and continue with the same process. What colors, objects, dimensions, and smells, etc. do you perceive through being the observer.

This is just a brief example of how to do remote viewing. To learn more, I recommend doing a course, even online. There are many videos on the topic out there. John Vivanco is a great person, among others, who you can go to and find out more. Below is an example of what's usually on printouts made for remote viewing.

Remote Viewing Template Sample

Name:

Date:

Time:

Target Reference Numbers

Ideogram

Textures:

Colors:

Smells:

Tastes:

Temperatures:

Sounds:

Dimensions/Motions:

How would you feel if you were there?

How would the site look if you were there?

AOL

Russell Targ and Harold Puthoff, who were parapsychologists at SRI (Stanford Research Institute) at the time, apparently created remote viewing – although it's said that Ingo Swan was the first to coin the term "Remote Viewing" in 1971. Ingo was well known for his remote viewing abilities.

Knowledge of the project being used by the U.S. government (known as "Project Stargate") was released to the public in the 1990s, causing the subject of remote viewing to hit mass consciousness.

Let's just say, however, even though the U.S. stopped Project Stargate, those "in the know" and from my own sources, I understand this is around the time that the U.S. government started to outsource their targets. This is still being done today; not with government oversight, although there is some talk of deep black projects still using it. Let's just say that I *know* this to be true.

I have included the subject of remote viewing here because it's part of initiating contact – although the method I recommend is free-flowing, compared to the one the U.S. government has used, even though there are similarities.

Most importantly, no matter what method you use, you will get results. It's all about choosing a method that works for you.

FREE-FLOWING REMOTE VIEWING

These next two methods of Free-Flowing Remote Viewing are techniques I came up with myself. Though many other people out there do similar techniques.

Imagine your body and mind as an antenna receiver (centralized in the pineal gland in the physical body), as well as a computer. Imagine that through the mind you are observing your breath and tapping into universal mind, or God's mind, which can be compared to the Internet. By understanding this, you will know how to tap into all that exists, anywhere in time and space, even across dimensions.

Once you start to practice remote viewing, take note of when you're correct during the process, and when you're not (after the fact). You might notice signs or feelings when your mind is making up information, or when you are spot on. It takes practice, and no one is ever 100% correct, but this is why working in groups is great – in the same way as practicing the CE-5 method. In a group, you can see what correlates with the results of others, and what doesn't. But don't throw anything out, because it might come to light later that some of what wasn't common in your group actually had some validity. Some of it won't, however. It's part of the art of practicing remote viewing.

After doing a clearing and then meditating, I go into what I call the "free flowing remote viewing" method. There are many ways you can go about this.

The intention is to connect, see what's in the area, or go out into space and discover what (or who) would like to make contact with you. If you are okay with it, allow the connection and then interact with who or what wants to communicate with you – not just through consciousness, but also in your location.

FREE-FLOWING REMOTE VIEWING METHOD 1

First, keep the feeling of love in your heart, do a clearing, and avoid trying to control what happens, because every time you practice remote viewing it will be different. The following is an example of how you might want to go into "free flowing remote viewing" with the intention to make contact. Use your inner guidance and intuition when doing this – always. Your target is to make contact in your location.

1. Do a clearing.

2. Enter the meditative state by following your breath.

3. Set the intention and send out a thought to make peaceful contact with those who are aligned with the awakening of humanity

and the earth. Invite them in to create a peaceful dialogue with you.

4. Now...set the intention and project out an invitation by thought to anything or anyone who is picking up on your thoughts. You might start to feel energy, get impressions and ideas, or descriptions of what any Beings in the vicinity might look like. Keep projecting thoughts. If you lock on to or feel another intelligence, it will likely project thoughts, concepts, and information back. You might even have a knowingness come through of who it is, what it is, and where it is from.

5. Find out how many different E.T. races or Beings are in your area. You can even project questions through thought, such as:

Why are you in the area? How do you live? What's your civilization like and what is your history?

6. You could even start initiating contact with an E.T. race or Inner Earth Beings that have a base in a nearby mountain or underground, and they might pick up on you.

7. You could invite them to make contact at a specific location. You might want to project and start visualizing that you are looking down on your location. Then zoom up and show the surrounding landmarks, mountains, and oceans by projecting it through thought and imagination.

8. Next...you might want to send out a though asking them what time you will be able to

see a sign that they are close by, and in what direction you should look: north, south, east, or west. They can sometimes show a sign straight away. This is a form of confirming contact if you get a time and direction ahead of time. If it occurs after remote viewing, say to the group, "They said (or I just *knew*) they would be in the east at 9:45 p.m." and then you will see a craft materialize or hover around, or a manifestation of an E.T vehicle in the location at the stated time.

FREE-FLOWING REMOTE VIEWING METHOD 2

This is a method similar to the one above.

1. Start by doing a clearing.

2. Set the intention to connect and go into a meditative state. Observe the breath and sounds around you, and connect to the mind behind the mind observing the breath.

3. Next, in absolute darkness, you might see the galaxy, if you set the intention to start from there. You might even see a craft in space or an otherworldly Being. From there, send out a thought inviting any Beings aligned with universal peace to connect, and then slowly visualize traveling back to this solar system.

First visualizing the earth, and then an aerial view of your location. This will show them your location, because your mind is connected to their mind. Then give it time, sit quietly, and simply observe your surroundings.

You might get results straight away, or it could take few hours. You might see nothing at all, but when you go to bed you might have an experience in your room or in your dreamtime. It's hard for them to come into our reality sometimes, they come through the best they can.

Some of you might want to do a clearing and meditate, and then connect to and through the intention for contact. Once you see them in your mind or feel their energy, you can start projecting questions through thought.

7. Connect with Your Spirit Guides and E.T.s

I have used many techniques and I always get results. Most of the time I do a clearing and observe the mind behind the mind observing the breath, and then I connect to universal mind. From there, I project a thought asking who or what is picking up on my thought and invite them to make contact – if it's safe to do so in whatever way they see fit. I take notice of any thoughts, ideas, epiphanies, knowingness, feelings, emotions, and sensations on my body, and then I let go.

Sometimes this works like a download. The analogy I use is imagine when a thought or a single word, concept, or idea/feeling comes through, to see it as a folder you are downloading off the Internet onto your computer.

Imagine that the name, thought, or idea is the folder name. Now…what happens when you click to download a file? The file appears on the computer, but then a download bar appears showing that it's downloading. So imagine the file name as the word or idea, and then let go, as all the information in the folder, (insight, guidance, information) now starts to download into your human mind. I understand from my experience that otherworldly Beings (or any Being, for that matter) communicate with us using telepathy/thought transfer. They send it from their mind – actually, from their light body, which is also called their "Merkabah" – and it goes through the unified field, hits your Merkabah, and then downloads into your consciousness. It happens quicker than the speed of light, although sometimes (depending on how much information they are relaying) it could take 10 minutes, an hour, or a day for all the information to come through. It's like books of information coming into you; it just depends on who or what the information is coming from and how much is being relayed using this form of communication.

Personally, most of the time, I just get a thought to go outside and look up and there is a craft in broad daylight. Sometimes Beings appear physically in my presence, in apparition form, in a column of light, or in a mist, and I start projecting thoughts and receiving thoughts, visions in the mind's eye, as well as sensations and feelings, all at the same time. It's important to take notice of feelings on the body such as static electricity, or like when you feel you are not alone, or you're in a room alone but feel like you're being watched. When you feel this way, you are sensing the light body of a Being overlapping your light body. The feeling of not being alone or feeling the energy is a physical manifestation of the light bodies overlapping.

Observing energy or watching for it is very important. As an example, let's say energy from a Being comes into your presence and you feel it on your right arm. Through the process of projecting a thought and asking what the Being looks like, you might get thoughts back in answer to your question. You might see what they look like with your eyes closed in your mind's eye in real time, or you might see a color, which might be the color of their light body.

Take notice of any feeling of energy on your body. Perhaps three weeks later you could be driving a car, making dinner, or whatever, and you might feel that same energy again. It's safe to say that 99% of the time when you feel similar energy in the same place, it may be the same being, and you know who it is. Start projecting thoughts and ideas to the Being as a way of communicating. Then let go and observe any images, ideas, thoughts, visions, or feelings that come up, because this is the way they will communicate back to you. Then just keep repeating the process.

You can even project a thought such as, "What's your name?" and then observe the names, letters, and imagery you receive referencing the Being's name. A lot of the time, they won't have a name, but they can make one up and they do have a sense of humor. If you are still and silent, you will notice each Being has its own frequency coming from their Merkabah. If you observe in silence, you might get a feeling and/or hear a humming sound; or you might hear a tone on a loop. Sometimes, when I have this experience, I mimic the sound or tone with a name (if they don't have a name) and use it to connect to them because it acts like a universal phone number.

We interact from a linear mind in mainly three ways to go trans dimensional (There are more, but I'm keeping it simple). Through projecting a thought to a sensation on the body, send a thought and you will receive communication back. When starting out, this will occur in one of three ways:

1. Through sensations. This can include emotions. Take notice of the energy and where and how it feels; it could even be all over your whole body.
2. Through thought, including ideas, epiphanies, ideas, concepts, and intuitive knowingness.
3. Through the mind's eye, including impressions, visuals, colors, and otherworldly Beings. You might see otherworldly landscapes, or you might even see inside a craft or beams of light, which are just on the periphery of Source/God itself.

Projecting thoughts, you'll receive answers through thought, feelings, and visuals. Again, project a thought, receive a thought, and repeat over and over until you feel the link has been cut off. This might last for 20 seconds, but you might receive heaps of information in that short time. You really don't need that long to do it; I do it in about 20 seconds, although for some of you, it might take 10 minutes or even an hour. Just go with what feels right.

Next is a method for connecting to your spirit guides or E.T.s that can also be used. I wrote about this in my book, *Connect to Your Spirit and E.T Guides*.

CONNECTING TO YOUR SPIRIT AND ET GUIDES METHOD

- Ask those who are aligned with the healing of the Earth and the awakening of humanity to connect to your consciousness.
- Ask the native spirits in your area and Gaia (Mother Earth), to connect to your consciousness. Also ask for their blessing to be here.
- Ask the nature spirits and elementals that are in alignment with you to connect with your consciousness.
- Now...ask your Guides, the Masters, Saints, Sages, and Beings you work with, and your own God Self to connect with your consciousness.
- Also ask that any psychic bonds and connections that are not positive to be

dissolved, along with any negative implants and attachments.

- Ask the healing energies to step forward and assist with any healing, physically, mentally, or emotionally that is needed.
- Let anything that is not in alignment with you be escorted by their Guides to where they need to go. Let them know they do not have to exist in their current state – because they are loved, healed, and forgiven.
- Now ask that Source, your own God Self, connect and assist you in reconnecting with your true nature, and help you learn, experience, see, and obtain the knowledge that will best help you at this time to help yourself and others.

Now take notice of your thoughts, feeling and visions, and follow this process:

- Put your hands on your lap with the palms facing up.
- Connect to energy on the hand you feel it on, or wherever you feel it on your body.
- Using thought ask the following:
  1. What do you look like? You might see a color, a visual of what they look like, an orb; a number of things might come through.
  2. What is your name or a reference for you? They sometimes make up names because they are coming from a higher state of consciousness. You might see letters, symbols, or words, or hear the tonality of their Merkabah as it resonates. Imagining this tone can be a way to connect with them in the future, just by thinking of it.

3. How are you connected to me? The Being might be part of your soul group, an old friend or family from another life, another aspect of you, a teacher, or a guide.
4. Where are you from? (Earth, Inner Earth, our solar system, another star system or galaxy, or even another dimension or an E.T craft?}
5. How do you assist me? Protection, guidance, etc.?
6. Do you have any messages for me?
7. Finally, using thought, ask any other questions you have.

Some people see otherworldly Beings in their mind's eye, and some hear and/or feel them. It's different for everyone. Just go with what works. It's a bit of a trial and error process to work out your own way of communication.

Some Beings use interdimensional technology that interfaces with thought. Some advanced Beings use pure consciousness with everything. They exist in their light body, and they might appear as a light in the sky or on the ground; they can also manifest in orb form. Some are in crafts; some crafts could be the size of our sun, bigger or smaller, but we only see them partially materialize as a small orb, compared to the size of their actual craft.

Some can appear in mist form. Sometimes they will land a craft in apparition form on you, a ghost-like appearance. They can even pull your consciousness onboard the craft while your physical body stays behind. It all depends on the consciousness of the race. I have photos of them like this. This is why sometimes ghosts or paranormal activity might actually be E.T.s or Angels. Even in the Bible, God and the Angels come in clouds in front of a person on the ground. Crafts and Beings appear like ghosts because they exist in a different frequency than we do.

I'm not covering everything here, because the subject is very layered, but I am bringing to light the core components I believe (after many years of personal experience) are the main ways to initiate contact and acknowledge it. It's simple at the heart of it, but it takes practice, inner work, persistence, and the drive to reach the goal of making contact.

8. Thought Projection Technique

Here is another simple technique that works, on occasion, for some people.

It's called "thought projection." While you are in a meditative state, sitting inside or outside in a chair, use your imagination to visualize a craft above you. Simply visualize the surrounding environment and a craft above you. You can do this for a few seconds, or a minute, and then take a break, or you can do it for longer periods of time. While doing this, project out the thought that you are open to connecting with those you are connected to on a soul level. You can also invite enlightened beings in.

You will be surprised by the results that might happen. Like anything, practice gets results.

9. The Pendulum Technique

Some of you might want to do a clearing and meditate, and once you feel the energy, use a pendulum to try and receive concrete information about when and where the Beings will make contact. Go through a process of elimination by asking questions such as, "What time will you arrive?"

Start by holding your pendulum and ask, "Show me a *yes*." It might swing away from you and come back in a repetitive motion indicating "yes." Then ask for a "no" and you might see the pendulum going left to right, indicating "no."

You can also get more specific, by asking, "What time will you appear, 3:00 p.m.? 4:00 p.m.?" Keep asking for a time until you get a "yes." This is an easy method to get answers about what or whom you might be able to contact.

Try going through the names of various E.T. races. Ask if there is an Angel or Inner Earth Being who might be willing to make contact.

Perhaps something from the past or future in the area might want to make contact. You might be able to contact one of many types of intelligent Beings, because when doing this, anything from anytime or any place can come through, whether local to your area, or not.

The most important thing to remember is it's all about intention and being in a state of consciousness in which you are able to make peaceful contact and interact with the Beings who show up. You must also be able to engage in peaceful dialogue with them. Don't try to control how it plays out. Just be open to whatever experience manifests.

10. Psychometry Exercise

Psychometry is when you hold an inanimate object and use your mind's eye, thoughts and feelings, to "read" the energy in it, including the history of events or people associated with the object. This type of spiritual practice is based on the idea that the energy and feelings of people and the events they experienced are imprinted on objects once held by them. Even clothing, furniture, and buildings can absorb energies and thoughts from the people and animals that have been around them. Joseph R. Buchanan, an American physiologist, first used the term "Psychometry" in 1842. He believed memories from the past are entombed in present physical reality.

Try this and see if you can receive information through thoughts, ideas, impressions, and feelings/knowingness. You can practice by asking someone for an object. Then hold the object and go into a state of meditation and observation. You can do this with anything, even something simple like another person's car keys.

11. Equipment and its Purpose

The equipment I am about to discuss is not "must have," but I am including it to give you an idea of the types of equipment that can be used when making contact to sense and document the events that occur.

For example, these devices can be used when filming or taking photos of crafts, E.Ts, anomalies, apparitions, and paranormal activity, some of which goes unnoticed to the human eye. Also, in a way, it brings science to documenting the unexplained — or what seems to be the unexplained at this time — including temperature changes and E.M.F. (Electromagnetic Field) readings from an unknown source. There is much that can be documented.

Electromagnetic, magnetic, and temperature changes occur as a result of changes in the environment for a reason, which can be either natural or paranormal, although the paranormal is actually normal. It might be a sign that something (or someone) is actually there with you and trying to communicate. So these devices are a way to pick up on whether there is a presence with you. Sometimes it helps to have various types of equipment to document your experiences, and sometimes you can even use them as a way to communicate with the paranormal, including otherworldly Beings. The best equipment is always your mind. Using equipment for documentation is extra.

Beware, though, because sometimes the Beings will drain batteries. It's theorized that they use the energy from the batteries in our devices (and even us, our energy) to manifest and/or communicate in the best or only way they can.

E.M.F. METER

An E.M.F. meter reads the electromagnetic field in the environment. It has been theorized that Beings manipulate electromagnetic fields in order to manifest. I have had an E.M.F. meter go off many times while I've been filming UFOs and when Beings are in my presence.

Sometimes, when having experiences, you might see the E.M F. meter light up (depending on the type you have). This can happen when seeing an apparition, or when having experiences like seeing orbs (balls of light), hearing disembodied voices, unexplainable languages, noises, being touched, or feelings of electrical sensations on the body, hearing unexplainable tones, and changes in temperature, or while seeing images in your mind's eye.

If you are using an E.M.F. meter, always do a base reading before contact by first scanning your own body with the device and the area you are making contact in. There could be power lines nearby or underground, which can give off a false reading. If you are in a house with bad wiring or electrical appliances, you might pick up high E.M.F.s. This is also why you need to turn off your phone and other equipment, because you don't want a false reading. So...try not to have the meter near other equipment, because E.M.F.s might register on the meter and you could end up thinking you're getting contact or an unexplainable reading, when, in fact, it can be explained. After a base reading, if you use your meter later and the reading goes higher, to a level that is not normal compared to earlier readings, it might mean that a Being or other paranormal influence is around.

You can also use your meter to ask questions and communicate with Beings by asking them to flash the lights or trigger the sound on it: once for "yes" and twice for "no." One of my meters is a K2. I like it because it is silent, which allows me to listen for anything else that might be happening when it lights up.

MAGNETIC FIELD (GAUSS) METER

A magnetic field meter, also known as a "magnetometer," can read and pick up changes in the magnetic field. Sometimes this means a Being is trying to manifest, or a craft is nearby. Its purpose is much the same as an E.M.F. meter, although the difference is that the E.M.F. meter reads the *electromagnetic* field, and the magnetometer (the Gauss Meter) picks up on the *magnetic* field.

Always do a base reading at a site before you do contact work, so you can tell if you are getting a higher reading than normal.

COMPASS

Compasses are great for a couple of reasons. First, you can use one to document the direction in which activity is occurring. Also, if it spins, freezes, or points in the wrong direction, you may have activity. With a compass, you can also determine any changes in the magnetic field. When this happens, it might mean a Being or craft is nearby.

GEIGER COUNTER

Geiger counters will give you a reading of any radiation in the area. With some reports of UFOs and landing trace cases, there is sometimes a high level of radiation that can affect people and the surrounding environment. Sometimes, years after an event, high levels of radiation can still be picked up when measured with a Geiger counter.

Basically you can use a Geiger counter like an E.M.F. or Gauss meter, so do a base reading before making contact. This way you will know a high level reading was not present beforehand. If you pick up a reading while making contact, you know it's unexplainable. Also, you can check it during an experience, so that from observation you can say there was a radiation effect when an event took place, if one, in fact, did take place.

On the other hand, black ops craft, ARV (Alien Reproduction Vehicles), or exotic military vehicles sometimes give off a radiation reading. Most of the time, E.T. vehicles are more advanced and do not use any form of nuclear propulsion, although I have seen cases where Beings have teleported to the ground and dematerialized. Later, when the area is scanned with a Geiger counter, very high levels of radiation can be picked up in the exact same place where the Being appeared and dematerialized.

NON-CONTACT THERMOMETER

These types of thermometers are good because they give you a reading straightaway and tell you the temperature in the atmosphere directly where you point the device. Just like with ghost hunting, temperature inversions can also be a byproduct of E.T. phenomena, when they are making contact or land a craft on you in apparition form. Sometimes, when there is a huge change in temperature, a Being could be nearby; even a craft might be closer than you think. Be logical when you use such a device, because there can be general and explainable reasons for a change in temperature. Is there wind, or not? Try to debunk the experience before saying anything is unexplained. Discernment is key, and it goes a long way in documenting valid contact. Try moving your hand around to define any area with a cold or hot spot, and then get out your infrared camera. You might capture something.

LASER

The type of laser you want to use (at the very least) is a wavelength of 532nm/405nm, which has a range of around 5 miles, depending on the type of laser – although these are illegal in some countries.

Lasers are great for more than one reason when you are trying to make contact. They make it easy to point out UFOs to others in your group, who might not be able to see them. Also, a laser is good when getting someone to point it toward the area of the E.T. craft, if you are using a camera already on zoom, or if it's a night vision monocular with high zoom, because you can just follow the laser up until you see the craft and start filming immediately. You might miss filming the action with a monocular or if the camera is in zoom mode after you've filmed a previous experience, so keep that in mind.

You can use a laser to communicate with a craft and ask it to power up. Sometimes the Beings can't see it, but some see a whole area at once, and/or they can connect consciously to you. They understand what you are trying to do, and they can see what you're seeing through your eyes, so they know what you're doing. Sometimes, if you flash the laser once, they will power up once. If you turn it on and off, twice in a row, they will power up twice in a row. There are many ways they can interact with you when you are using a laser. You can do a similar thing with a high-powered flashlight or car headlights. Doing this shows interaction between you on the ground and them in the sky. Make sure your type of laser is legal in your country or state. Also, having someone designated on the laser might be easier; an excess of people with lasers can also create problems.

WARNING: DO NOT POINT A LASER AT SOMEONE'S EYES, AT HELICOPTERS, OR AT PLANES OR OTHERWORLDLY BEINGS.

BINOCULARS

Binoculars are a great tool for getting up-close views of objects in the air, or to check out the surrounding environment for activity.

For example, you might hear noises in a direction or see lights far in the distance. When using binoculars, you might be able to find out if the activity is explainable, such as people camping, cars, etc., if the area has enough light to see.

DIGITAL AUDIO RECORDER

Many ghost-hunting teams use them for catching disembodied voice phenomena. This type of recorder allows you to ask questions, and when reviewing the recording later you can hear a response. The same technique can be applied to CE-5, although you might not get a human voice, but rather something spoken in an unknown language or star language. You might capture a number of things, such as a clicking noise, the humming sound of a craft, or tones. A digital recorder is a great device to use. You might even get a series of beeps or coded messages that are mathematical in their response, depending on what (or whom) you're interacting with. You might even hear unexplainable sounds, but if you can capture them on the recording, the unexplainable sound might be evidence. Evidence of what? Well...even if you cannot explain what you heard, going through a process of what it is *not* can provide evidence of unexplainable phenomenon. Also, time-coding the recordings is great, because it provides a record of the time and date the event took place, in case something does happen.

NIGHT VISION CAMERA

Night vision cameras are great. There are many on the market, although most are only good at capturing events local to you on the ground and not in the sky, although some pick up the stars. Infrared is part of the electromagnetic spectrum, and it's just outside the range of what we can see with the human eye. It can also pick up what we do see. It's a great device to have, because you can see in the dark with it when you look through the viewfinder, and you might catch something that is near you, but that you cannot see with your naked eye. From Beings to crafts, to orbs, this will help you capture some of what's around you. If you sense something is in the area, or even if you are just looking through the viewfinder, you might be surprised what you end up capturing. Just make sure you get it on record.

CAMERA

Cameras are great for capturing evidence. Sometimes taking photos in the dark without the flash on opens the chance for what you capture to be more unexplainable, because using the flash can sometimes make bugs, dust, and other debris in the air appear unexplainable, when, in fact, they can be explained. You might see unexplainable light sources, Beings, or crafts appear in your photos. Of course, you can use the flash if you want to; either way, you can capture evidence. A lot of the cameras available these days allow you to record video, too, and although some cameras are great for photos, they are not as good for recording video. If you sense something, take a photo or a series of photos; you might end up with something interesting. Just remember, the higher the pixels, the better the image quality. Also, if your camera also records video, the better the optical zoom, the better the images and the closer you will be to recording the phenomena. A lot of the time, if people take a photo of the sun or other light source, a lens flare can appear as an anomaly for those who don't know how cameras and light work. So be aware of this, too.

DIGITAL VIDEO RECORDER

These devices are great to use for a number of reasons, including recording crafts, orbs, Beings, and witnesses to events. Using a video camera is crucial to capturing evidence. It's best to get the highest quality you can. 4k are popular these days. They are basically 4 times HD, which is approximately four times more pixels than a HD camera. Go for good quality and good zooming capabilities. Just be careful with the zoom when filming UFOs. Sometimes a craft will appear in the footage, not as it actually is when zoomed up too much, because the sensor in the lens creates a diamond effect. So just watch how close you zoom up. It is best to use this type of recorder with a tripod, if you can, although sometimes the crafts are overhead and they can be hard to film when you are using a tripod.

The best camera, in my opinion, is the Sony A7s2, which I use these days, although for a fraction of the price, the Sionyx Aurora is a color night vision camera that's very affordable, under $1,000. I usually carry this around on me, as well as other cameras.

Just remember, the better the optical zoom, the better the footage and the closer you will be able to get to the phenomena, craft, or Being.

NIGHT VISION MONOCULAR

These devices are great when starting out, and they are low cost, around a couple hundred dollars. They have a lot of zoom, but most don't record audio and the quality isn't good on some.

Just a little tip: don't turn on the infrared light, because it only helps illuminate objects close up.

It does not, however, affect the monocular's performance because what you are filming is at a distance. Turning off the infrared light will save your battery power, too.

INFRARED SCOPE

These are very useful. They are basically scopes that allow you to see in infrared. The military and law enforcement use them, and there are different generations and quality. Generation 1 (GEN 1) is the lowest quality, but now they are up to GEN 3. Some have an adapter, so you can connect a video camera to them and film, which is how most people in the CE-5 community have been filming for years.

ALL-SKY CAMERA

These can be found on the market more and more, and they are also becoming more affordable. From what I have used and seen, they use a fisheye lens that captures the whole sky, so you can just sit back and not worry about filming.

Just make sure that if you buy one, it has a day *and* night function. Some new ones automatically zoom in on objects if the sensor picks up something; otherwise, you will just get a distance view. In other words, what your eyes can see is what you'll get.

UV (ULTRAVIOLET) CAMERA

These great cameras are basically like the Infrared digital video recorders and cameras, although they are able to capture images and videos in the ultraviolet spectrum, which, again, we cannot see with the naked eye. Cameras are also available that have both UV and Infrared in one.

THERMAL IMAGINING CAMERA

These are epic devices. Basically, they work like (and are) infrared, but they turn the heat signature of people and the environment into color in order to make what you view more noticeable. Some of them can see through walls (plumbers use them to identify any blockages in pipes). I have a Seek Thermal brand one that plugs into a mobile phone; it costs only a few hundred dollars. There are a few different brands and types on the market.

DRONE

After initiating contact and flying a drone around, you might end up capturing some evidence. I have seen people accidently capture footage on them, although not on purpose. I don't use drones because they are noisy and distracting.

WALKY-TALKY

These are great to use with a team in case anyone gets separated, or if you want to send a team member into an area to look for activity, and when you want to make sure the activity is not explainable.

SATELLITE TRACKER

Using a satellite tracker is a must. Usually I have one person on it watching out for activity. If anyone sees anything, we tell him or her the direction and location. If it's not on the tracker, there is a chance it might be something anomalous. Sometimes crafts can appear like a satellite. A lot of the time crafts first scan a group from high up, although you want to see reactions from the laser, unconventional maneuvers, and other anomalous activity from the object, which further shows it's not a satellite.

There are many types of apps and websites. Just look around, see which ones work great for you, and keep an eye out for the space station or Star Link, because they get mistaken for UFOs. Also watch out for iridium flares, which occur when a satellite seems to change in size or flashes. These flares are actually the sun reflecting off the satellite. This can also happen a few hours after sundown and a few hours before the sun comes up, depending on your location.

With this said, an Internet connection is needed, unless you print a chart out first. Keep the person on the tracker a little away from the group so you don't get a reading on your E.M.F. meter, because this can happen when using phones that are not turned off or are on airplane mode. You might want people to take turns on the tracker.

PLANE TRACKER

There are many apps and websites that track planes; however, an Internet connection is needed unless you print a chart out first. Though a chart won't always be accurate because flights keep changing all the time. Keep the person using the tracker a little away from the group so you don't get a reading on your E.M.F. meter, which can happen when you are using phones that are not turned all the way off. On top of this, many people who are new to CE-5 mistake planes for UFOs, because they are not used to looking up at the sky. Sometimes a plane's landing light (if it's turned on) can make the plane appear as an orb, although most people start to recognize the tell-tail signs of what planes look like, depending on how far away they are. Sometimes they hear them, too, as they spend more and more time sky watching.

SPACE WEATHER

Knowing about and checking for local meteor showers and other space weather events is great, too, because sometimes meteors and other space weather can appear as paranormal or UFO activity, when, in fact, it's explainable. I usually go to spaceweather.com. This site is really good for getting updates on the amazing stuff that's happening and what I might be able to see, including things like meteor showers.

PLANET TRACKER

Using an app or going on the computer to check where different planets are is something you should do for daytime sightings, although people sometimes mistake planets for crafts at night. There are cool apps and sites that show the names of stars and constellations, too. Now...there are times when you might think you're seeing something anomalous, but on rare occasions you can see planets during the day, as well as at night; so be aware of this.

LED LIGHT

These are great to use if you need to see in the dark. Most have multiple settings for the intensity of light, which is great, because you don't want lights on unless needed. You want to be in darkness at night; your eyes will end up adjusting. Sometimes the light from the screen on a camera or phone is enough to see.

INFRARED LIGHT / BEACON

Unseen to the eye – and due to E.T.s and Beings sometimes being able to see in that spectrum, or due to their technology being able to pick it up – you might want to get a high-power flashlight and put an infrared light lens over the light, or use a high-powered infra-red flashlight. Put it in the middle or away from the group, and point it up into the sky. You won't see anything unless you look at it in infrared, but it's great to help the Beings pinpoint where you are and make contact happen quicker. This is not a must, however, because they will always find you, anyway. Contact has everything to do with consciousness.

RADAR DETECTOR

I don't use radar detectors myself, but years ago when there was a CE-5 event held for me in Queensland, a person brought one. You can get communication back with tones and beeps through them as a form of communication. Mainly, from what I know, the radar detectors used for checking car speeds are the type used. The devices used by E.T.s can set off the radar and communicate through them. For example, like an E.M.F. meter, you can ask questions and get one beep for "yes," and two beeps for "no."

WEATHER APP

You can check the weather on your phone or computer. These apps are good for knowing what the temperature is, or if the sky will be clear. Of course, you don't want to get caught up in a storm or flood, or other adverse weather conditions.

TRAIL CAMERA

These are used a lot for hunting, but they are also great for CE-5. Most have a motion sensor that triggers the camera to start recording. If your camera has infrared, it can be used during the night. These are great to point at a group during meditation or in any area where paranormal activity might be happening. Most trail cameras are not great for capturing activity in the sky, but they are great for down low.

There are most likely other devices I have not covered here, or that I don't know about. I have only discussed tools I have personal knowledge about. Also, new devices, including better cameras, are always coming on the market for ghost hunting, and they can also be used for CE-5.

12. Filming Techniques

I have to add here some tips and tools I wish I had known about years ago, because I had to figure them out on my own, especially when filming during the day.

First, sit in a lawn chair, but if you're the one with the camera, you want to be in the shade or have your back to the sun. Doing this and wearing sunglasses reduces glare and makes it so much easier to see something in the sky. You would think it's easier to see E.T. crafts in the sky during the day, but sometimes the blue sky makes it so all you see is blue. These crafts can appear as balls of light or rainbow iridescent morphing lights.

You might also see a shadow made by the craft, which can make it look dark or black, this is the bottom of the craft. In this case, you may see the sides, or the top of the craft stand out when the sun reflects off it. Clouds can make it easier for your eyes to focus when looking up into the sky, but if it's a clear sky, look up and try to focus as high up as you can. Sometimes looking at the sky in a defocused type of way can make it easier to see crafts.

If you are looking towards the sun part of the time, hold up your hand to block the sun and look around your hand. You would be surprised how many times I have seen crafts in this way, hiding in plain sight near the sun.

Be on the watch for flying saucers, geometric iridescent crafts, crafts changing shape, cigar-type crafts, triangular crafts, and/or balls or egg-shaped crafts. There are many other types; they come in all shapes, sizes, and colors. Some might appear white or metallic, and sometimes they are pure light. Some are structured from what I call "living light." There are many types of organic crafts, which are Beings in their Merkabahs (light bodies).

With all this said, use a tripod when you can, although sometimes it's hard to film using one if the craft is directly overhead. Sometimes you might need to move, which can make filming harder if you are using a tripod. I film using a tripod, but most of the time I use the quick release and I pull the camera off; this way I can still film under certain conditions.

Also…try to move around and line up branches, power lines, or buildings in your viewfinder, and align these objects a few inches away from the craft. Then, when you start filming, it will be easier to film the craft, because you know where it is specifically or in what general area. This is due to sometimes having problems with the object not being seen on the viewfinder or screen on the camera. If you are aware of where the object is, position your camera in line with it, press record, and slowly zoom in on it. If this doesn't work, zoom out and zoom in quick on the craft's location, and you should be able to pick it up. A lot of the new cameras are great, but their manual focus acts like an auto focus, which is different from older manual cameras.

Filming at night is a lot easier, especially when using infrared or color night vision, or the Sony A7s2. Note that the bigger the lens, or more zoom on the camera, the better.

When filming, sometimes you might get a diamond, and you might think that's what the craft looks like. This can be the result of zooming in too much, so back up a bit and try to film the object as clearly as possible.

13. Our Stuff, Their Stuff

I have to add something here that some people don't often think about: sometimes you will see our "stuff," which might include exotic military crafts, black ops crafts, or deep black crafts, including crafts under USAP (Unacknowledged Special Access Programs) and/or SSP (Secret Space Program), plus drones. The list of possibilities goes on and on.

When exploring connection with E.T. crafts, look for a consciousness connection to them. You might feel blissed out when this happens.

WARNING: Break any connection immediately if you get a negative feeling, because you might have encountered reptilians, certain types of greys, and/or PLFs (Program Life Forms), which mainly look like greys. There are covert groups that do abductions for a number of reasons. With that said, if it looks more "nuts and bolts," it might be of human origin.

There are remote viewers and devices the covert groups use for tracking people in communication with otherworldly Beings. So...this is just a heads-up regarding possibilities. Sometimes you might see jets following UFOs. I have seen this a lot in Australia and at James Gilliland's Ranch ECETI in Washington State, as well as other places in America.

Sometimes covert groups can even infiltrate your group, which has been done to many UFO groups, on occasion, for the purpose of gleaning information and other purposes.

It would be irresponsible of me not to mention these things, because they can and have happened to many others and me over the years, meaning military and covert groups spying, infiltrating, and/or monitoring these types of events. Sometimes they might stage an event to set you up, so they can have you and your evidence debunked later on.

During these types of interactions, black ops and other entities are following E.T. crafts. They might be trying to capture them or shoot them down using electromagnetic pulse weaponry, scalar technology, and other forms of exotic technology. There are a number of reasons for their being around, in addition to monitoring. Don't focus on this or worry about it. Just be aware.

If you see a presumed craft, look at it carefully and see if there is any propulsion you can identify. Are there any unexplainable maneuvers? Does the craft make any noise? Can it blink out or move at high rates of speed instantaneously. Check your feelings and determine if the craft can react to your thoughts. In these ways, you can judge whether what you see is our stuff or their stuff, by which I mean E.T.s.

14. Physical Evidence

As a head's up…whether seen or not, sometimes crop circles will appear and also landing marks from a craft, before, during, or after you go to a location and connect with otherworldly intelligences out in the field. This phenomenon shows more than what meets the eye, which can happen during CE-5.

Orbs sometimes appear low on the tree line, hovering around the trees. They might leave singed marks on the trees or burned leaves as evidence. Also, the tops of tree branches might be broken, which is also a sign of a paranormal event. Thus, in their own way, they again leave you with a form of confirmation and evidence.

Crystals and stones can be left for numerous reasons. They might appear around you, in your pocket, or on the ground at your feet, sometimes as a gift or as confirmation of contact. Even objects you might have lost years earlier can appear out of thin air or in your pocket. This is a way of letting you know they made contact – in their own weird and wonderful way.

For some, small scoop marks, pricks, or dots can appear on one's body, and in some cases, forming a triangle or constellations on the body can appear after contact. Sometimes these marks can be a form of upgrade to the body, or a check-up type physical this can be linked to. There is probably a lot more, but just be aware of these types of potential events.

At my own events, sometimes people with health issues are spontaneously healed. This continues to happen to this day, and, so far, the health issues have not come back for some. Strange and wonderful things can happen as the result of a CE-5 experience.

15. Crafts and Beings Appearing in Ways You Might Not Expect

Contact is not always what many people believe or expect it to be. A lot of the time, a craft can land on you in your bedroom in apparition form, like a ghost, or over you and your group, whether inside or outside. When this happens, you might hear and feel a humming sensation going through you.

This happens on occasion: When you close your eyes, you might see the Beings in your mind's eye and inside the craft itself. Sometimes with your eyes open, you might even see the Beings and the craft looking ghost-like, although most see this in their peripheral vision. It's theorized that the peripheral vision picks up more of the visible light spectrum and what the eyes don't see when directly looking ahead, because the cones and rods in the eyes see more of the visible light spectrum.

To add to this, if you are outside or in the field making contact and this happens, you will see something misty-looking land at a distance from you, or on you and your group. Again, in your peripheral vision (or your mind's eye) you might see the Beings, although some people can see them in apparition form when looking directly ahead (like myself). A change in temperature is very common, too.

So many times – when it has been very cold at night and we are doing CE-5 in a group – and then we could feel the temperature change dramatically, becoming beautiful, like being in the tropics, this could mean contact is taking place. If and when this happens, you can simply walk out of the mist or the area that has gotten dramatically colder or warmer. If you feel the temperature change and don't see the mist, walk until you feel the original temperature, and then start walking around, staying on the borderline of both the warmer and cold temperature. In this way, you can, basically, work out the size and dimensions of the craft.

Take photos if and when this happens, or film in infrared, and you'll be surprised by what you capture. I see this a lot and have captured craft landing on the ground or down low, and the Beings in it in apparition form. I've seen this many times with witnesses present – all of us in awe about this aspect of making contact. It's not the nuts and bolts concept like most think. Otherworldly Beings can and sometimes do appear in physical form in the group or around the group, or in my case, in my home or wherever I am. Sometimes they phase in and out, as if they are using a type of teleportation technology.

There are safety measures they go by, and also a mandate they have to follow, meaning they are not allowed to stray too far from the diplomatic and universal law perspective.

They can be seen in apparition form, and even in the physical state. You can also see E.T crafts fly into mountains, the ground, water, or even coming out of these areas. I have seen this happen many times, and I have also seen them zooming through forests.

16. Types of E.T.s and Beings

There are many types of Beings, below is a basic, brief overview list of what's common. Know that some of these Beings don't need a craft; they can travel around in their light body, also known as their Merkabah/Light Vehicle.

E.T. RACES

- Andromedans (From the Andromeda Galaxy)
- Andromedans (Could also mean - from the Andromeda Constellation)
- Lyrans (A Constellation)
- Sirians (Part of the Constellation Canis Major)
- Orions (The Constellation Orion)
- Pleiadians (A star Cluster part of the Constellation Taurus).
- Arcturians (A star part of the Constellation Bootes)

- Apha Centurians (A Star in the Constellation Centaurus)
- Cruxians (Crux Constellation)
- Pegusians (The Pegusus Constellation)

This is just a brief overview of some of the Being's locations and human terms for them. There are many different types of Beings from each area, just like there is a vast variety of life on earth.

ANGELS (Celestial Light Beings)

- Metatron
- Michael
- Gabriel
- Ariel
- Raphael
- Uriel
- The Elohim (Our God Self, although there are different variations that left Source, as well for different purposes.)

This is just a brief overview - there are many other Angels as well.

LIST OF OTHER BEINGS

- Inner Earth Beings (Some connected to Atlantis and Lemuria, as well as others connected to off-world Beings).
- The Guardians – These tend to be keepers and monitors of portals.
- Gaia (Mother Earth)
- Fairies
- Elementals
- Nature Spirits
- Original Spirits (Aboriginals, Native American Spirits).
- Plant Spirits
- Animal Spirits
- Humans from the future
- Humans from the past
- Spirits of the deceased

THE LOWER LIGHT

- Reptilians
- Reptilian Greys
- Draco Reptilians
- Serpent Beings

- The Archons (Fallen Elohim)
- Parasitic Thought Forms
- Demonic Entities

ASCENDED MASTERS

- Jesus
- Buddha
- Kwan Yin
- Padmasambhava
- Mary Magdalene
- Mother Mary

There are many more as well, to many to mention.

RAINBOW LIGHT BODY BEINGS

- Ascended Beings

"SOURCE"

- God, the Creator, the Source of all things.

Part 3

Making Contact

17. Preparation: Location and Doing it Alone or as Part of a Team

You can initiate contact at any time, day or night, individually or in a group, although a group can be more effective. There is no requirement for a set number of people, but having a small contact team of between 5 to 20 people is good. You want the group to be on the same level as much as possible and willing and able to work toward having a cohesive collective consciousness.

Anyone who just wants to see crafts or other phenomena, or who has doubt about the reality of CE-5, can hinder the contact experience, because they are there for the wrong reasons. Also they can mess with the energy of the overall group. Don't get me wrong. I understand people want to see something, but when initiating contact it's about taking things to the next level, initiating peaceful contact, and creating a dialogue with the greater family of man.

For some, you might want to make an expedition out of it, perhaps a two to five-day camping trip.

During the day, you can remote view and meditate, and keep an eye out for phenomena. At night, you can sky watch, while going back and forth between remote viewing and meditation. Basically, you want to get to the point where you can remote view and meditate in an active, awakened state. In this state, you will know when and where to look, while taking notice of changes in the environment around you, such as temperature changes, sounds, or changes in the atmosphere.

If you are planning a night trip, a good way to go about it is to arrive at your chosen location in the middle of the afternoon, unpack everything, have some food, talk about intention, and set up any equipment you might want to use. Then get into it!

If you have not been out to a particular location before, when you first arrive, look around for hazards and get to know the place while the sun is still up. You don't have to do this, but it will increase your confidence later, because you can avoid stumbling around in the dark.

Some people think I'm out all night looking for crafts, but I know what time to go outside and see them, both during the day and at night. I have been vibrated onto crafts and have physical, and/or mind-to-mind interactions with them. This happens during the day and night, basically, anywhere at anytime.

CE-5 takes the explorations to a new level. Yes, I experience this stuff all the time, and many do, but doing it in groups takes it to the next level. It all has to do with everyone being open-minded, not in a state of negativity or fearful reactionary mind, and setting the intent for a peaceful dialogue.

You don't have to go out into nature, although it's definitely better. I have had crowds of 100 to 200 people in parks located in cities, and we get results during the day and night as a team. A lot of my own evidence is captured during the day in the outer suburbs of Melbourne, Australia, as well as every other place I have lived or visited, whether in the country or in a city. So you don't even need to go out of town or out of a large city. Just pull up a seat in the backyard and initiate contact. Keep an eye out and take notice of thoughts, sensations, and images in your mind's eye.

Now...if you pick a location for a trip, choose a peaceful environment with good vibes. You can do CE-5 from home, like I said, or out in the bush, anywhere. But each location will have pluses and minuses.

For example, in town or the city you have light pollution, commercial and military aircrafts, noise, and other distractions, and most of the time a limited view of the sky. So if you do it from home, and your home is situated in a town or city, these are the factors you will have to deal with.

If you decide to go out-of-town, pick a location with a huge view of the sky, open and with limited distractions, minimal aircraft activity, and away from noise. It might be land that has been considered sacred by those who lived there, going back a long time. When arriving at any location, always ask the ancient spirits of the place, using thought or out loud, for permission to be there. You will be able to tell by thought or by feeling whether you are welcomed, or not.

Also state your intention. You might interact with an ancient civilization or Beings that also came to Earth long ago, or those who are from other worlds and/or might be residing in a different dimension.

It's also important to respect the land. Don't leave rubbish lying around; just try to leave the area as you found it. Sacred sites have good energy, which is why the ancients picked those areas and deemed them sacred. Some are portal areas. Some areas might be where otherworldly beings have a base underground or in a mountain and unseen by us. Sometimes, by thought or simple knowingness or intuition, you might be led to a particular location, and it might be a form of communication from something that's picking up on your intention and wants to make contact.

The downside of being out-of-town is that in case of an emergency, (like someone getting hurt), you are a bit away from getting help. Also, you won't have power for equipment or toilets out in bush, so take this into consideration.

Either way, make sure the place you pick is safe from hazards. I recommend that if you do this by yourself, it's best to make contact at home or in some other safe location, in case you have an accident. If you go out to a location, make sure there are two or more of you, in case something unfortunate happens. If you must go alone, be sure to let someone know where you're going and when you will be back.

I have to add here that you might want to remote view or do a contact meditation before going outside or to the location, if you are going out in the field. This can help you set your own intention and/or help with the intention of the group if everyone does this. You might even receive insight on when and where activity could happen.

Most importantly, when entering or arriving at a location, ask the land, Gaia, and any native spirits, Beings, and nature spirits for a blessing to be on the land. Out of respect, state your purpose for being on the land and ask for permission.

18. Safety and Hazards Check

When picking a location, at home you are pretty safe, but when you are out-of-town, it's best to investigate the location beforehand, during the day. There might be hazards like holes in the ground, uneven ground, or wild animals such as snakes or whatever wild animals live in your area. So, get familiar with the location you pick, because you could hurt yourself in an accident or get bitten by local wildlife.

Always keep a first aid kit and a cell phone close by, but it's best to keep the phone turned off during contact work so there is one less distraction, and so it doesn't interfere with your devices, such as E.M.F. meters. There might be no reception in the area, so make a plan B in case of an emergency. Also, if you are far out of town, identify the location of nearby hospitals and other emergency personnel, in case you need help. Before leaving, let your family and friends know where you are going.

19. Tips and Tools

First off, make sure you have proper clothing and footwear for the time of year, and if you are going out-of-town or into the city take blankets and spare clothing. Also make sure you take an Esky or flask with hot or cold drinks, water, food (so you can keep up your energy), and cooking equipment, if you think you might need them. Take plastic bags to put your rubbish in, as well.

If you take medication, or need something like an asthma inhaler, make sure you bring it. Also bring mosquito repellent so the bugs don't eat you alive (if you are going to an area with mosquitos). Some repellants contain awful chemicals, but there are some good natural ones out there, too.

Other "must have" items include a camping chair and maybe a table, if you think you'll need it. Sometimes it helps with being able to keep an eye on your equipment and keep track of everything if it's all in one place, such as on a table. A flashlight (with new batteries) is also a must have, so that when you need light you'll have it. And in some cases, take toilet paper and a shovel...if you know what I mean.

Also, get to know what's usually in the sky at the location where you're going; use the available apps. Take notice of airplane flight paths and planets, and also go over what's north, south, east, and west of you, so if you communicate with the person on the satellite tracker, it will be easier for both of you to determine whether what you're seeing is a satellite.

I highly recommend getting and using a satellite tracker app. They are great for real time ISS (International Space Station) and satellite information.

Also, do some research to get acquainted with the different types of natural phenomenon that some people mistake as UFOs so you know what to ignore.

Finally, you might want to do research and get to know your night sky, meaning planets, stars, and constellations. This can be fun and educational, and it can help you pass the time between sightings and interactions.

20. Setting Up Your Equipment

When setting up equipment at a location, whether at home or out in the bush, it's not that hard; just think about what's practical.

You might want to designate a main area near where you will be meditating and sky watching. Make sure you have plenty of room and can get away from trees and buildings. In this way, you will be able to get a good view of the sky in all directions, away from anything that can block out the view of the sky.

If you are working in a group, put the chairs in a circle so everyone attending the session can monitor the entire sky. Place cameras in an area where you can pick them up quickly. You might want to have someone on a camera that's running at all times, because sometimes the crafts might not be around long. Also, make sure people don't get in the way of others with cameras.

Keep a flashlight on your person or in a specific place, so when you need light, you'll have it close at hand. Also park the car a good distance away from the group so you have plenty of room to see in the distance on the ground, in case anomalies such as orbs, apparitions, or even Beings pop up. Try to be free of clutter and keep food and drinks away from the main area as much as possible.

PREPARATION CHECKLIST

- Pick a location. (You can remote view or meditate on it before choosing your location or going to it.)
- Pack your equipment, food, water, and chairs, etc.
- When you arrive at the site, ask permission from the land and any associated Spirits to be there.
- Check for hazards.
- Set up your equipment and chairs, etc.
- Connect as a group. (This might be by doing energy work together, having an "Om" circle, etc. See next chapter.)
- Start meditation / free flowing remote viewing.
- Now that you are in a heighten awareness state, be on the lookout for contact.

21. Energy Work: Connecting Mind, Body, and Spirit

Once you have set up, and before or during sundown, you might want to do some energy work to help connect your mind, body, and spirit. This can also help everyone in a group connect.

Anything such as Yoga, Tai Chi, or Qigong can be useful. Just do whatever method you enjoy. Connecting as a group will help you get connected with your energy and make everyone flow as one, and also help the energy of your being, your physical body, and your mind get focused. Of course, doing this alone is fine, too.

Make it fun, have a laugh about it, and get all participants on the same page if in a group. Doing energy work together will help everyone in the group connect. Laugh about the process, muck around, have some fun with it, while also respecting each other and the practices.

22. Initiating Contact

Now...if you are in a group, you might want to get in a circle and hold hands (if you feel comfortable doing so). Of course, not holding hands is okay, too. Then do a group clearing (solo if you are alone). Ask any enlightened Beings to connect with you, in whatever form they want to do so, for the purpose of universal peace and easing humanity into a dialogue with the greater family of man. Do this only if it feels safe and if everyone present wants to. Do this your own way and come from the heart when inviting the Beings in. Focus on learning more about them, their way of life, etc., but don't try to control it or any experiences that might arise. Just go with the flow.

In a group or alone, you might want to visualize a beam of light going up into the sky, while holding the intention of love and your willingness to connect. You could even ask everyone to chant the sound "Om" together. You might think this is funny, but the E.T.s like this vibe. You might even want to set up an offering in the middle of the circle with flowers and crystals, etc.

After doing whatever method you choose – the ones suggested above or your own method from the heart – maybe play a singing bowl. This is great as a prelude to the start of meditation and remote viewing, because crystal bowls can be of great assistance in connecting with universal mind, Simply focus on the sound of the bowl and then observe your mind – the space *behind* your mind – as you listen and observe the sound of the bowl. Personally, I can do this in a second by focusing on ambient sounds in the environment or a singing bowl.

You can go about all this in your own way; it's just great to do something to bring a group together as one when starting out. This is part of the process of being one with yourself and others while initiating contact. You don't have to use any of these tools and tips. Just do whatever works for you and your group.

If you want to make contact individually, just invite the Beings to you, in the same way as mentioned above. You can skip the group exercises if you wish. It's up to you. One person I know imagines a big neon green hand coming up out of his body and going way up into the sky. He invites the Beings in this way, and they often respond.

If tuning into the Beings, you might find there is a soul connection between you and them a lot of the time. It might be from other lives, and you have had more than one life amongst the stars. All of us have incarnated in different star systems many times. The only time this is not the case is when a Beings has come directly from Source.

Over many years, when making contact in a group, I have noticed that if you have (as an example) many people in the group who have been Pleiadians in their past lives, some of their present time interactions will be with the Pleiadians.

23. CE-5 Contact Meditation and Remote Viewing Method

Whether by yourself or in a group, you might decide to start with a meditation. Some of the people in the group might want to have one person do a guided meditation to connect the group even more.

During this time, be aware of any thoughts, impressions, ideas, sensations on the body, or even images that might come in through your mind's eye. These might include Beings and their crafts, or you might appear to be inside a craft. You could even become aware of being out in space.

Go with the first thing that comes to mind and let go of any doubt. You might get the thought "north," which could mean look to the north, because you might have actually received the thought, "We are coming from the north." You might think "9," which could mean that at nine o'clock you will see activity. Next, start your remote viewing after the meditation is over.

You can even focus on going into space and inviting the Beings back to your location by projecting this thought, and then visualizing your location and project it out. Some of you might want to focus on the area near you and invite in anything aligned with what you're doing. Even your spirit guides or star family can come in. Take notice of any thoughts, imagery, or sensations.

Next is a meditation method you might want to use if you don't have your own method. This is basically a clearing and a way to invite the Beings in. Remember... after meditating, remote viewing and clearing, enter into a state of observation. Observe any thoughts, visions, feelings, and emotions as an answer back from any thoughts you put out. Keep repeating this until you feel the communication has stopped.

EXAMPLE OF HOW TO MAKE CONTACT USING MEDITATION & REMOTE VIEWING

Start by visualizing a color or feeling that is therapeutic, loving, and revitalizing for you.

Next...as you breathe out, relax the muscles in your face around your eyes, cheeks, jaw, and neck.

Breathe the loving energy in again, and breathe out any tension in your shoulders, back, arms, and stomach.

Breathe in the loving energy again, and breathe out any tension from your hips down to your toes; then keep breathing the loving energy in, and breathing the loving energy back out.

Next, I always go into another clearing method, just for safety precautions. You can say this out loud or think it, or even create your own method.

- "We ask that any cords, attachments, parasitic thought forms, implants, anything not aligned with the awakening of humanity and the earth, and that is not here for the purpose of peaceful contact to be dissolved or escorted to their perfect place. Go now in peace." You might want to imagine in your mind that you and the group are engulfed in light.

- "We ask for the healing energies to step forth, and to go through the molecular structure of our bodies and organs, our emotional bodies, and the light body as a whole, balancing out, enhancing, or rectifying any unwanted energies to help the mind, body, and spirit connection run at optimal efficiency."

- "We now ask for a blessing from Gaia, the original spirits of the land, nature spirits, elementals, plant and animal spirits, inner earth Beings, our star families, the Angels, and the beautiful many (for Beings that are not thought of) and Source."

- "We now ask that we are sealed off in our own dome of protection, immune from any outside influences, and that only those who are positive and would like to make contact for the purpose of universal peace please do so, if it is safe to do so. In peace."

- Now…continue to meditate and do the free-flowing remote viewing method, as long as you feel like it. Put out thoughts and ask questions, see what thoughts, ideas, feelings and visions come back as answers.

- You may want to ask…

1. What is your name?

2. Where are you from?

3. Why have you come through?

4. Are you connected to me or anyone in the group?

5. How can we assist you and how can you assist us?

6. Any Messages?

7. Would you like to show yourselves?

At this time, and during the meditation, you might want one person to keep their eyes open so they can look around for activity. So many times when I have started to meditate, even in a group, the Beings don't want us to focus on meditating, because they want to interact straight away. They are more than ready to make contact.

Tell the people in your group that if they have any thoughts about a time or direction in which activity will occur, they need to speak up. Often a few people will get the exact same information, which means there was contact, because the activity will happen at the time, or in the direction, they got from the communication. I have done this many times. You may even get thoughts on who the Beings are and where they are from, even messages may come through.

If people are feeling sensations on the body, take a photo of that person or persons. Something might appear. At the start of the outing or while meditating, I recommend there be someone whose job it is to keep taking photos, if possible. Also they should tell the group when they are taking photos, if they are using a flash. This way the participants will have a chance to close their eyes so the flash doesn't affect their sight when they go back to darkness.

24. What to be on the Lookout For

1. Distortion of space and time – this might look like heat coming off a road on a hot day.
2. Orbs (balls of light)
3. Being touched – but nothing is there
4. Objects moving for no reason
5. Unexplainable lights
6. Sensation of energy on the body
7. Plasma light down low or up in the sky
8. Flashes of light
9. See-through crafts in apparition form
10. Thoughts that are not yours
11. Misty type apparitions around you that could be crafts or Beings
12. Fully materialized Beings and/or crafts
13. UFOs
14. Change of atmosphere/temperature

15. Equipment failure, battery drainage, static on viewing screen or any devices, or activity and readings on devices
16. Be aware of people in the group that aren't part of the group, as sometimes the Beings teleport down and then disappear.

Sometimes, when doing contact work, a craft will land on you or your group. I have experienced this myself. You don't notice it unless you notice the energy change or the atmospheric change in the environment. Also, the sounds in the environment becomes sort of muffled, different. When this happens, you can literally see the craft – it will look transparent, misty, like a ghost. Many people do not pick up on this because they are unaware, or they think they are seeing fog or some other natural phenomena.

You can walk straight out of it, away from the group. Then, when you look back in your peripheral vision at where you just were, (and sometimes when looking straight ahead) you can see the ghost-like craft, but with a definite outline. If you walk back into it, you might see the Beings directly or in your peripheral vision; or if you close your eyes, you might see them and where you are in your mind's eye.

Take notice of your thoughts during CE-5, because this is how the Beings communicate: through thought, as well as visions, feelings, and sensations on the body.

25. Examples of Contact Evidence

Now we are going into some photos and snapshots from videos I have taken to give you an idea of what to look out for, or what you, yourself, might capture when making contact.

These images have been analyzed by Jason Gleaves and are just a small sample of my evidence from over the years.

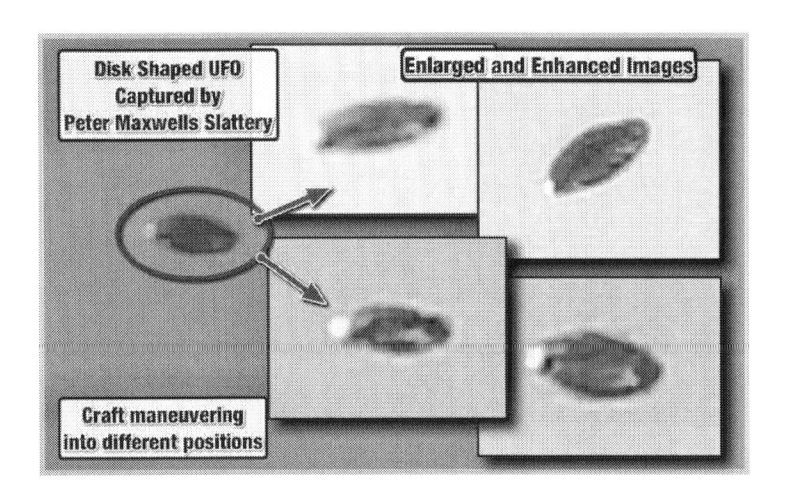

154

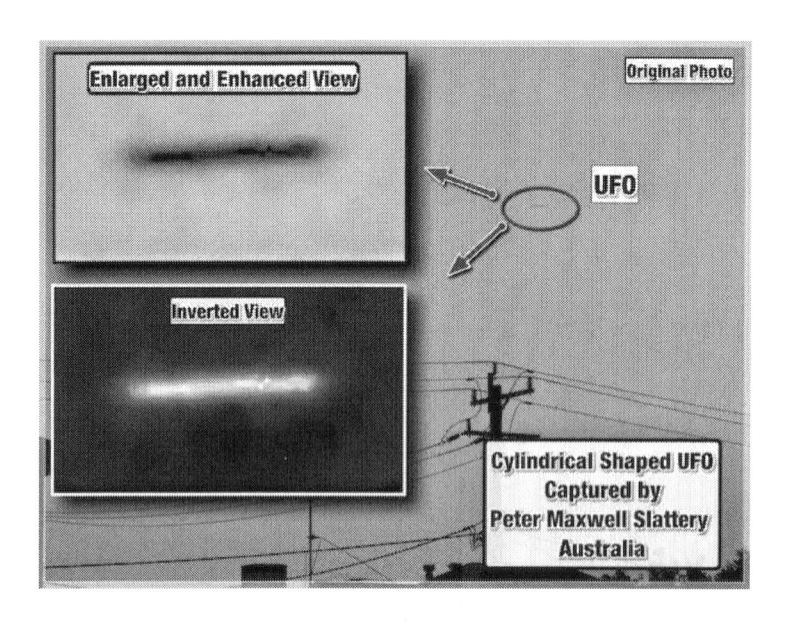

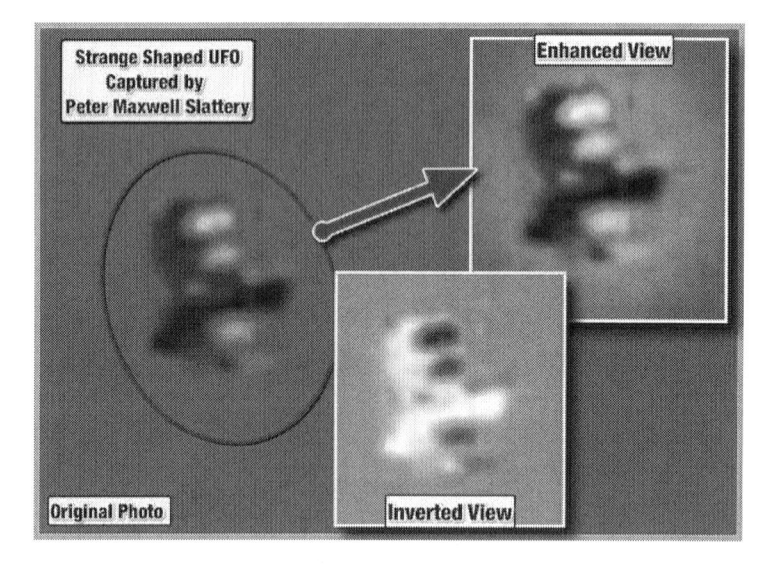

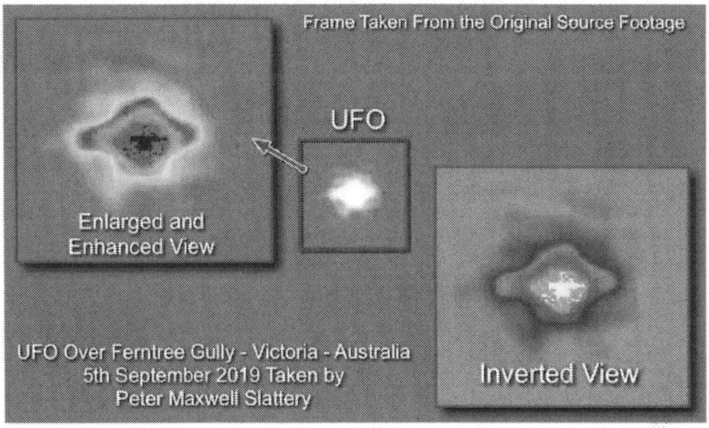
Frame Taken From the Original Source Footage
UFO
Enlarged and
Enhanced View
Inverted View
UFO Over Ferntree Gully - Victoria - Australia
5th September 2019 Taken by
Peter Maxwell Slattery

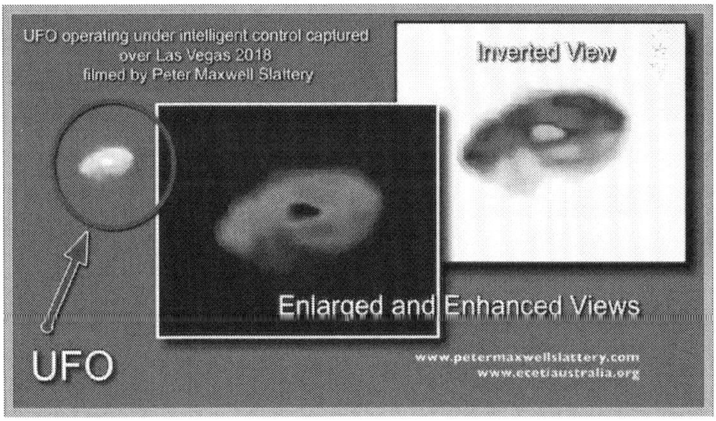
UFO operating under intelligent control captured
over Las Vegas 2018
filmed by Peter Maxwell Slattery
Inverted View
Enlarged and Enhanced Views
UFO
www.petermaxwellslattery.com
www.ecetiaustralia.org

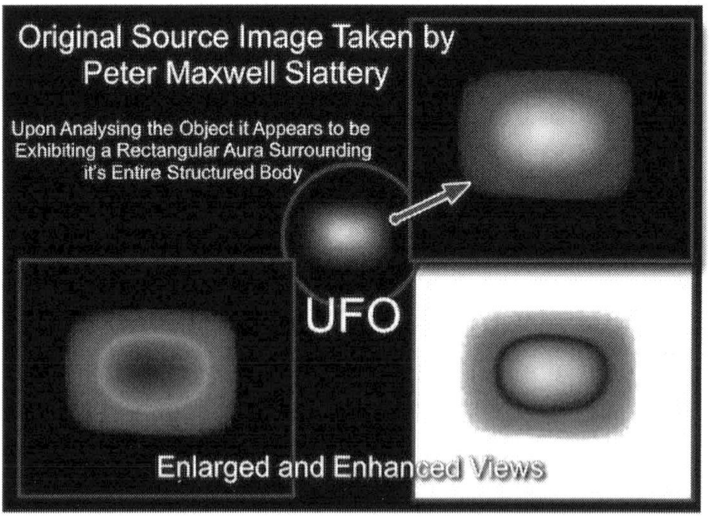
Original Source Image Taken by
Peter Maxwell Slattery
Upon Analysing the Object it Appears to be
Exhibiting a Rectangular Aura Surrounding
it's Entire Structured Body
UFO
Enlarged and Enhanced Views

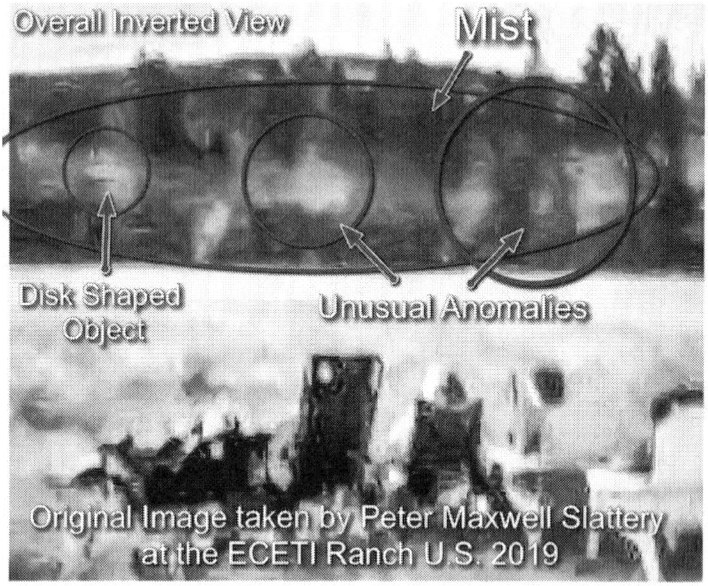
Overall Inverted View
Mist
Disk Shaped
Object
Unusual Anomalies
Original Image taken by Peter Maxwell Slattery
at the ECETI Ranch U.S. 2019

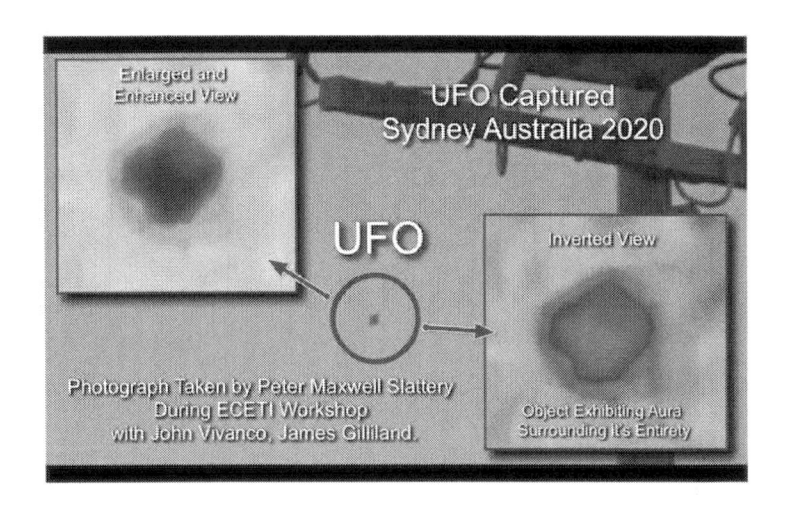

UFO Captured Sydney Australia 2020

Enlarged and Enhanced View

UFO

Inverted View

Photograph Taken by Peter Maxwell Slattery During ECETI Workshop with John Vivanco, James Gilliland.

Object Exhibiting Aura Surrounding It's Entirety

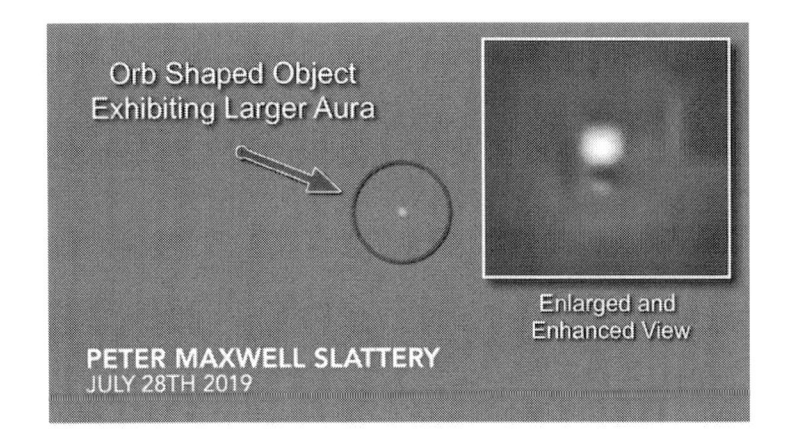

Orb Shaped Object Exhibiting Larger Aura

Enlarged and Enhanced View

PETER MAXWELL SLATTERY
JULY 28TH 2019

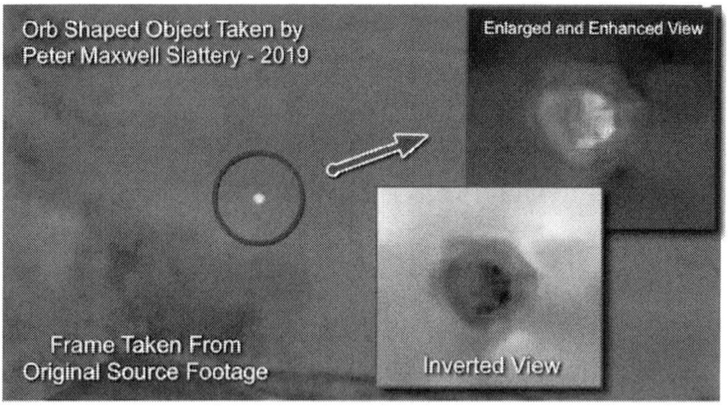
Orb Shaped Object Taken by
Peter Maxwell Slattery - 2019
Enlarged and Enhanced View
Inverted View
Frame Taken From
Original Source Footage

Disk Shaped Object
Captured Over Australia
by
Peter Maxwell Slattery - 2020
UFO
Enlarged and
Enhanced View
Original Source Photograph

Enlarged and Enhanced Views

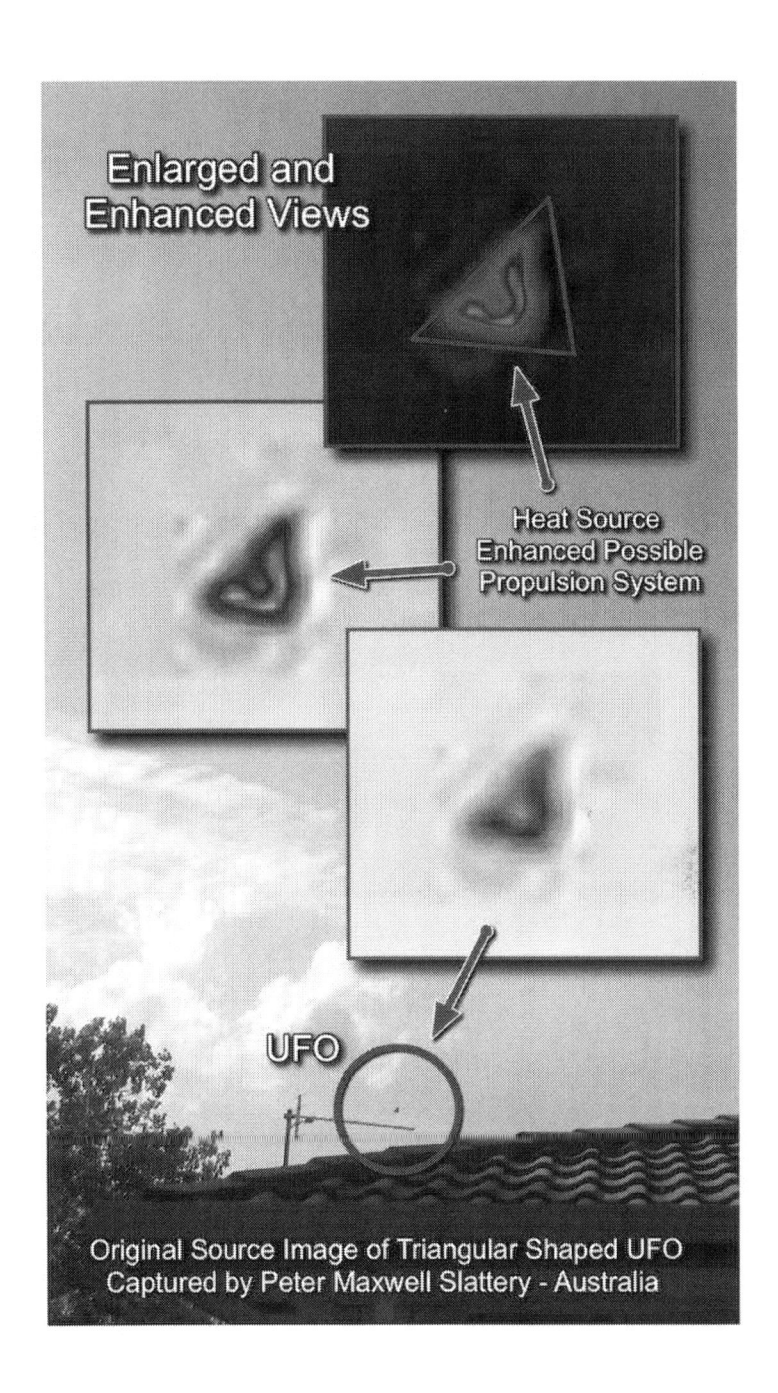

Heat Source Enhanced Possible Propulsion System

UFO

Original Source Image of Triangular Shaped UFO Captured by Peter Maxwell Slattery - Australia

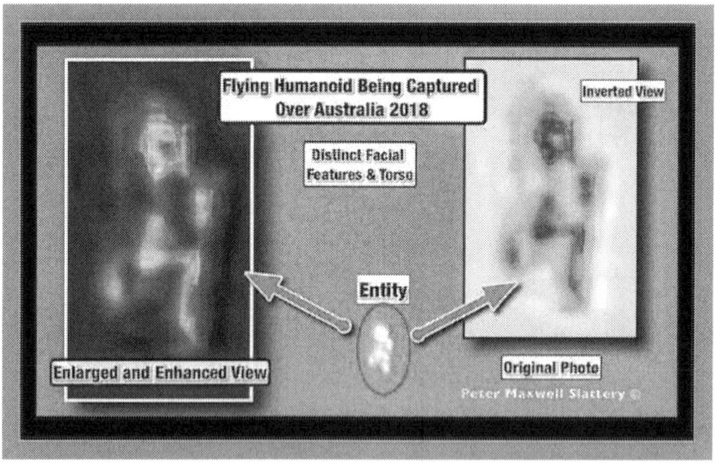
Flying Humanoid Being Captured
Over Australia 2018
Inverted View
Distinct Facial
Features & Torso
Entity
Enlarged and Enhanced View
Original Photo
Peter Maxwell Slattery ©

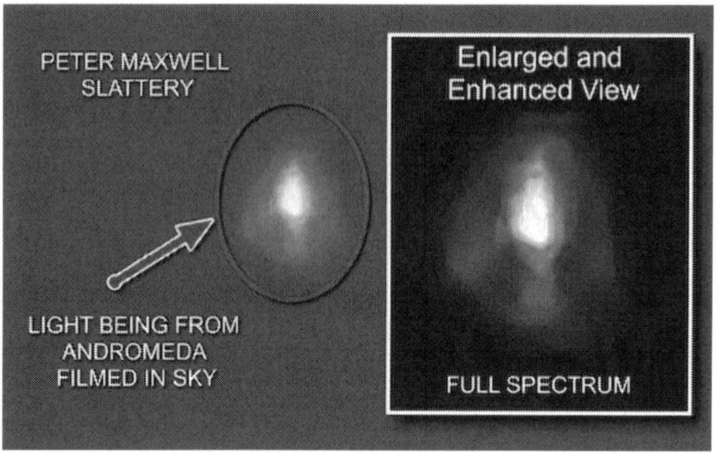
PETER MAXWELL
SLATTERY
Enlarged and
Enhanced View
LIGHT BEING FROM
ANDROMEDA
FILMED IN SKY
FULL SPECTRUM

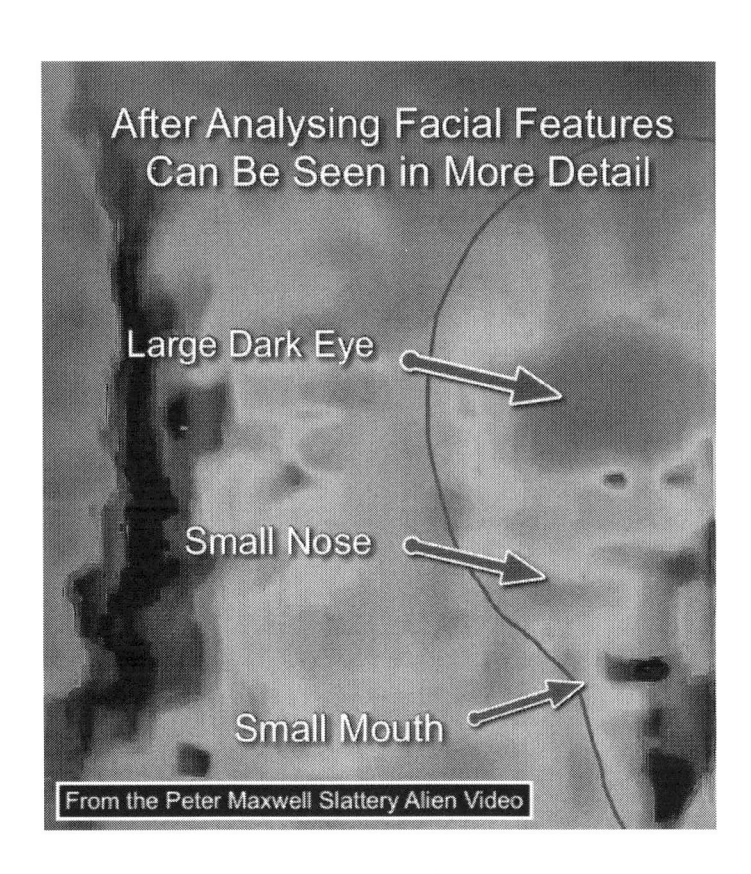

After Analysing Facial Features Can Be Seen in More Detail

Large Dark Eye

Small Nose

Small Mouth

From the Peter Maxwell Slattery Alien Video

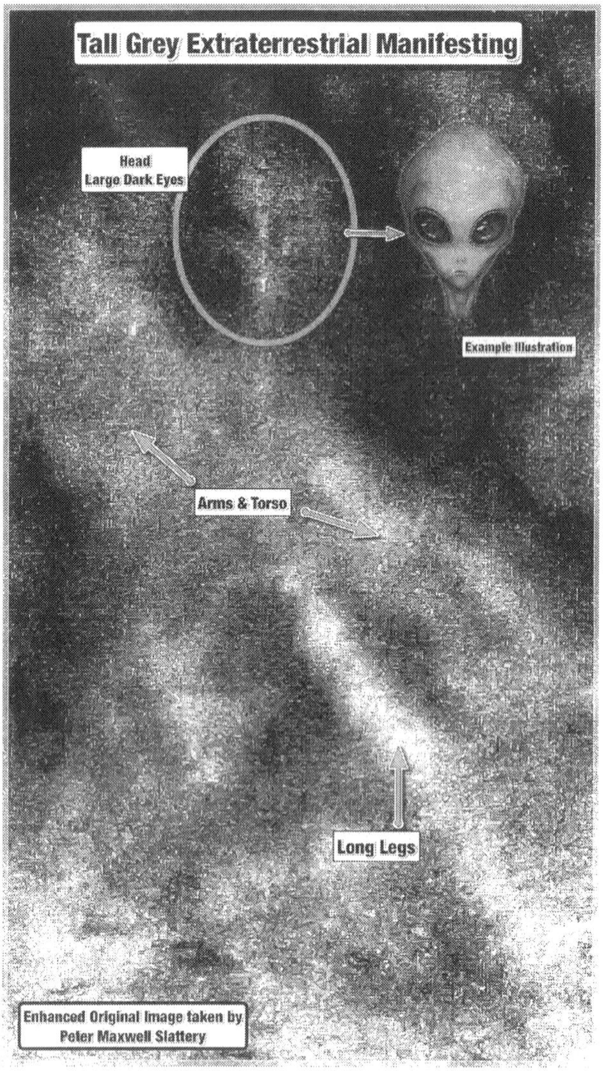
Tall Grey Extraterrestrial Manifesting
Head
Large Dark Eyes
Example Illustration
Arms & Torso
Long Legs
Enhanced Original Image taken by
Peter Maxwell Slattery

26. Ending Your CE-5 Session

In the end...actually, there is never an end to contact and multidimensional mind. It continues on and on into infinity.

When finishing up a group session, you might want to connect again by holding hands and chanting "Om" while standing in a circle. You can also offer a big "thank you" to who or whatever connected with you that night.

In addition, try to remain aware, because sometimes after leaving a location, contact can take place when you are back inside your home or when you are going to sleep. You might see apparitions or flashes of light in your home or wherever you are staying. Beings might materialize in and out of your location or room. Even while falling asleep, you might see a Being in your mind's eye. It will look like a dream. You might even fall asleep and dream you are onboard a craft with otherworldly Beings. This is so much more common than most think; it's simply the way some of these Beings interact with us. And it will continue, whether you are doing CE-5 or not. The contact is never truly over.

In the end, the most important practice is your intention to connect with these Beings. Come from a place of love, and most of the time your interactions will be with friends and families from your other experiences and incarnations.

In a way, this is just the beginning of CE-5, as you open the door for continuous contact on a recognizable level, especially if you keep up your practices of meditation and clearing. This path leads more to connecting you with who you truly are, beyond an E.T concept, because you are an aspect of Source, God, the consciousness that we are all a part of. From there, through synchronicities, events, and your journey, your mission will become more and more clear.

This experience is no more than just a dream. Gods lose themselves to refine themselves again, and you are in that process now. Each person wakes up when they are meant to. Just remember...the keys are love, an open mind, and being in a space of love. The journey has just begun, as we as a collective and as individuals reawaken to who we really are.

In comes down to basics, just ask, and you will receive, whether its contact, guidance, or direction. Everything is just a thought away.

27. Final Note

I hope this book has been informative and given you an idea about how to initiate contact, whether you are already an experiencer, or not. Actually, I believe everyone is to some degree, even if on a very subtle level.

The rest is up to you. Have fun with doing CE-5, but remember, in following this path, you are an Ambassador to the Universe and beyond for the human race. Respect this, take pride in it, and do it with a loving heart, good intentions, and an open mind. The results, knowledge, information, and experiences will be amazing.

The future is unknown and continuously being created. Our reality is created from within. Change within and it will project outside of you. Know that nothing is set in stone, even though there are possibilities. In the end, know you are the creator of your reality and you can do anything you set your mind and heart to creating.

Let the light inside each and every one of you shine.

Books by Peter Maxwell Slattery

The Book of Shi-Ji

The Book of Shi-Ji 2

The Book of Shi-Ji 3

Connect to Your Spirit and ET Guides

Awakening: UFOs and Other Strange Happenings

Operation Starseed: A Temporal War

About the Author

Peter Maxwell Slattery is an international bestselling author, and he is known as an E.T contact experiencer. His E.T experiences started at an early age and continue to this day, with hundreds of witnesses to events.

Pete's experiences have been detailed in an overwhelming amount of photographic and video evidence related to UFOs, otherworldly Beings, and apparitions, which have been analyzed by Jason Gleaves (Ex-U.K. Air Force and Aerospace), and remote viewed by John Vivanco (*The Psychic Spy*) and his group, which has worked for the FBI. Pete's story also includes physical trace evidence.

Pete's experiences with extraterrestrials have led him to help people and groups make ET contact themselves, in addition to healing and tapping into their own abilities.

He has appeared on History Channel's *Ancient Aliens* and *Paranormal Caught On Camera*, Channel 7's *Prime News,* and *Sunrise,* and many other international television programs. He has made worldwide news, been in numerous documentaries, been written about in magazines, and has been a guest on mainstream radio shows, including *Coast-to-Coast*. Pete is also a musician and, as a filmmaker, he has made a number of documentaries on the subject of E.T's. He was featured in *The Cosmic Secret*, which was a number one documentary film on iTunes in 2019, and James Gilliland's *Contact Has Begun 2*. Also, his UFO footage was featured in *Close Encounters of The 5th Kind,* which was also a number one film on iTunes in 2020.

Peter Maxwell Slattery continues to open the world up to the greater reality that "We are not alone" and that "We are all amazing, powerful Beings."

For more information, go to petermaxwellslattery.com

Follow Pete on Facebook, YouTube, Instagram, and Twitter

Printed in Great Britain
by Amazon